MOMENTS CRISTIANO RONALDO

by **CRISTIANO RONALDO**
with **MANUELA BRANDÃO**

photography **JORGE MONTEIRO**

MOMENTS TO DEDICATE

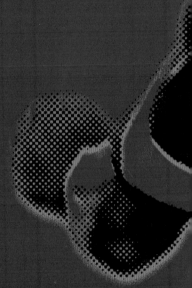

The title sums up the essence of this book, these are moments from my childhood, and they tell how much football enraptured me, from a young age. These are stories of a child who abandoned everything for the pleasure of playing with a ball. These are, in fact, slices of the experiences I have lived up to now. Some of them left me glowing with joy, such as the first time I was selected to train with Sporting's professional squad, the first game with the first team, my first international appearance, my transfer to Manchester, the trophies I have already won. And a lot more. Other experiences were traumatic and led me to despair and tears, such as the period during which I had to live alone at Sporting's training centre and could not bear the homesickness for my family and friends. Or my father's death, a wound that has still not healed.

This book is dedicated to his memory, for he is still present in my life and I know that, wherever he is, he will still be as proud of me as he always was, pride which he enjoyed announcing to the world. This dedication extends, in the same proportion, to all the members of my family: my mother, Maria Dolores, my siblings, Elma, Hugo and Cátia, my brother-in-law José Pereira and my cousin Nuno Viveiros. They are all that is most precious to me. It was largely because of them that I decided to embark on this adventure, for they were the ones who persuaded me to share with you a small part of my experience of life.

My mother still treats me as if I were a baby. I, Cristiano Ronaldo, like to see myself as a kid. I will always fight to stay a kid, even when age states the contrary, for only in that way I believe is it possible to face life's adversities more light-heartedly, with more optimism, whilst preserving a readiness to learn and improve. Always. That is how I act every day, whether in casual situations, or in my professional capacity. To improve as a human being, to value myself as a football professional, and to contribute even more to the success of Manchester United.

I hope you appreciate these "Moments" of my life as much as I have appreciated them. For this book is my image, reflected in the mirror of my soul.

I can recall without any problem the first time I saw Cristiano Ronaldo in action. He was playing in a youth tournament in Portugal and I was lucky enough to have been watching the match on television. Here was a singular talent, so much so, that he made me sit up and take notice.

I decided there and then to keep an eye out for the youngster to see if my first impression had been accurate or that I had seen him put in an exceptional one-off performance.

The sight of this precociously talented youngster with the lightening pace and equally quick feet eventually, inexplicably, faded from my thoughts, but they were rapidly reignited when Sir Alex Ferguson brought him to Old Trafford from Sporting Club Lisbon. Cristiano had played against Manchester United in a pre-season friendly in the Portuguese capital and made such an impression on the United players that they urged Sir Alex to sign him, whatever it cost!

He made his debut, as a second half substitute, against Bolton Wanderers and was an instant hit with the Old Trafford crowd, who, it has to be said, know a little bit about the game. His brief appearance in the side was captivating and he immediately became a firm favourite with the club's supporters.

It took Cristiano no time at all to establish himself in the Premiership and he quickly went from strength to strength under Sir Alex's careful guidance. Football supporters adore exciting players who possess flair and individual ability, and Cristiano certainly slots comfortably into that category.

Already an integral part of the Portuguese national side, he had a fine 2006 World Cup in Germany, but was caught up in that controversial incident, involving Wayne Rooney, which had England supporters up in arms. He had to expect a rough ride when the new season began, but a new Cristiano emerged from jeers and boos as an even more accomplished professional. The derision quickly evaporated as the people who had sought to deride him realised that their efforts were merely inspiring the Manchester United winger.

Manchester United proceeded to claim their 16th league championship, with Cristiano instrumental in that success. He had silenced all the critics who expressed the view that he wouldn't be able to handle the pressure from the England fans, and I even suspect that some of them harboured a grudging admiration for the youngster as the season reached its dramatic climax.

It has been a pleasure to watch him over the past few years and I look forward, with relish, to future seasons and witnessing Cristiano's development into an even more exceptional player.

We at Old Trafford are proud that his future is to be at Old Trafford, which can only be good for the club and equally beneficial for Cristiano, a truly great talent!

Sir Bobby Charlton

MY NAME IS

CRISTIANO RONALDO . . .

. . . AND I KNOW THIS NAME MEANS A LOT TO THOSE WHO LOVE FOOTBALL – THE GREAT LOVE OF MY LIFE. THEY KNOW ME VERY WELL . . . WHENEVER THEY SEE ME ON THE PITCH, THEY KNOW HOW I PLAY, HOW I DRIBBLE; THEY UNDERSTAND MY STYLE – BUT THERE IS A LOT ABOUT ME THAT NOBODY KNOWS.

MY YOUTH DOES NOT GIVE ME THE RIGHT TO HAVE MY LIFE STORY PUT INTO WORDS, NOR DOES THIS BOOK INTEND TO REPRESENT IT. THIS BOOK IS NOTHING BUT AN INVITATION TO THE READER TO SHARE WITH ME SOME OF THE MOST FANTASTIC MOMENTS OF MY CAREER, UNTIL NOW. SO, THIS IS NOT THE FULL STORY OF MY LIFE. ONE DAY, IN THE VERY DISTANT FUTURE, THAT WILL BE WRITTEN, AS HOPEFULLY GOD WILL HELP ME BUILD A CAREER SUFFICIENTLY FULFILLED TO WRITE IT . . . IN A BOOK WITH MANY MORE PAGES!

I intend to dedicate a large part of that book to the Manchester United victories, to the club that really made me famous, and turned me into a football idol at only 22 years old. I will never forget United, for its strength, for the pleasure I have in wearing their shirt.

This pleasure can be compared only to that of wearing the shirt of the Portuguese national football team. I want to share with you some very curious stories: I will tell you about my childhood, the hard times I had leaving my home island of Madeira when I was only a boy, to move to the Portuguese mainland. And I will also tell you about a word which is ours, with no translation in the whole world, apart from Portuguese: "saudade" (to miss).

Today, I do not feel that any more. My life has made an extraordinary turn. I am privileged to be playing football, for being in the Manchester United team as well as in my country's national football team. I am privileged because I do what I enjoy – and they even pay me for it. As you will understand through all the "moments" written in this book, the ball has always been a great friend of mine. This has been my main attraction, ever since I had to jump over my neighbours' garden fence to get it back, when playing with my friends in the streets of Funchal.

As I have already said, this is a book comprised mainly of moments: some funny, some sad – too sad . . . like coping with my father's death.

I hope that by the end of these sundry stories you will get to know Cristiano Ronaldo better, at least a little better . . . As you finish reading the last line I hope you will reach the conclusion you have enjoyed these pages with the same enthusiasm that you would follow a well dribbled football. I always mean to please others.

Then you will see if I am a good storyteller or not. The images are a great help and the reader can rest assured that, one day, the book of my life will finally appear; but meanwhile I want to keep on unlocking the pages of that book on the pitch, especially in England wearing the Manchester United shirt, or on the world stage where Portugal play. Nobody can blame me for loving my country so much, nor for giving Manchester United such a very special place in my heart.

THE BOOK OF MY LIFE

I FEEL SO LUCKY,
DOING WHAT I
LIKE THE MOST . . .

THE PLANE HAD JUST TOUCHED DOWN ON THE COMODORO AIRPORT RUNWAY IN DILI. I LOOKED THROUGH THE WINDOW AND I COULD NOT BELIEVE MY EYES. A SMALL CROWD WAS PATIENTLY WAITING FOR MY ARRIVAL, WITH CAMERAS OR CAMCORDERS IN ONE HAND AND WHITE PIECES OF PAPER OR WELCOME POSTERS IN THE OTHER. IT WAS IMPRESSIVE, BUT THIS WAS NOTHING WHEN COMPARED WITH WHAT WAITED FOR ME DURING THE REST OF THE DAY I SPENT IN THE CAPITAL OF EAST TIMOR. THE STREETS WERE FILLED WITH THOUSANDS OF PEOPLE. THEY ALL CAME JUST TO SEE ME, TO WAVE AT ME, TO GET A SMILE, A GREETING, A WORD, AN AUTOGRAPH, A PICTURE OF ME.

TIMOR

I was moved. I was impressed with the great interest of that entire population in me. The Timorese had probably never before been that close to a football player from the Portuguese national football team or Manchester United. I know that Timor and Portugal do have a crossed historical past, and I also know that the Timorese love football and this great passion is the only thing capable of explaining such great enthusiasm during my visit to Dili. Whenever Portugal is playing, they wake up at dawn and turn on the TV to enjoy the excitement of the game (due to the time zone, on that side of the world they are nine hours ahead of Portugal and England). For instance, that was what happened during Euro 2004: a great success for our country both in the organisation and our sporting participation, although with a sad and frustrating end for those who worked so hard and deserved to win the European Championship. Despite this defeat, the Timorese were proud of the way we fought, as they are like brothers to us.

2005

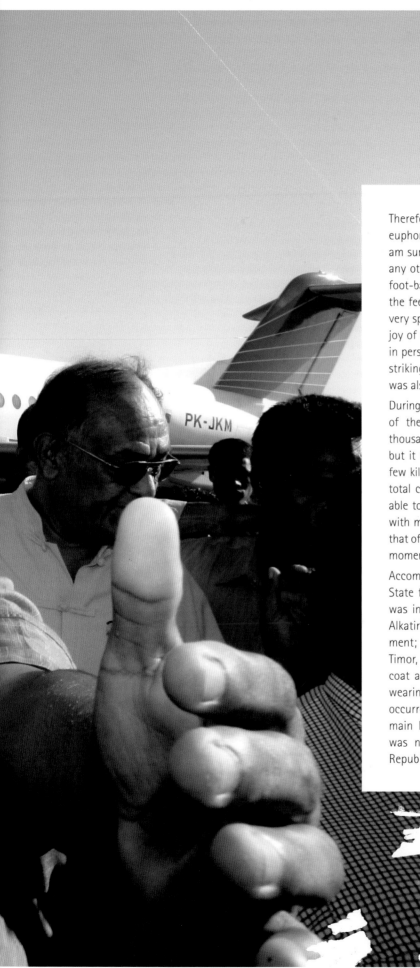

Airport at Díli,
Timor

Therefore, there was no surprise to see the euphoria caused by my presence in Dili, and I am sure the same would have happened with any other member of the Portuguese national foot-ball team. But right now I am talking about the feelings I had myself. I felt, undeniably, a very special person. To see and experience the joy of so many people who wanted to see me in person was enough. It was one of the most striking and intense experiences of my life. It was also one I will never forget.

During my drive in a jeep up to the residence of the prime minister, Mari Alkatiri, I saw thousands of people. It was a short distance, but it took me more than an hour to cover a few kilometres. In the streets of Dili there was total confusion and not even the police were able to scatter the crowd, who were euphoric with my presence, shouting out my name and that of Portugal. Impressive. It was one of those moments that give you goose pimples . . .

Accompanied by Laurentino Dias, Secretary of State for Youth and Sports of Portugal, who was in Timor on an official visit, I met Mari Alkatiri and several ministers of his government; for instance, the Minister of Sports of Timor, who surprised me when he took off his coat and asked me to sign the shirt he was wearing. One of the most intense moments occurred when I met Xanana Gusmão, the main leader of the Timorese resistance, who was now the President of the Democratic Republic of East Timor, and we embraced each

IT WAS ONE OF THE MOST STRIKING AND MOST INTENSE EXPERIENCES OF MY LIFE

THE MINISTER OF SPORTS OF TIMOR, WHO SURPRISED ME WHEN HE TOOK OFF HIS COAT AND ASKED ME TO SIGN THE SHIRT HE WAS WEARING

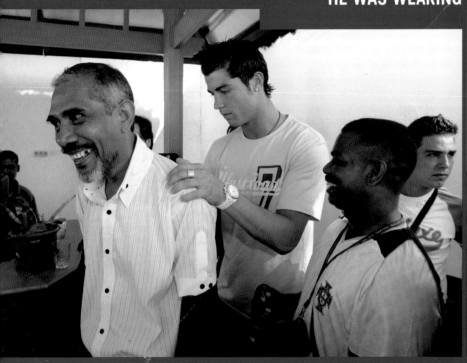 

other with vigour. As a kid, the little I knew about Timor did not mean much to me, but the name of Xanana was familiar to me from my youth, as he is an outstanding and exceptionally courageous man. It was very interesting, not only for the symbolism of personally meeting someone of such importance in shaping the history of this young country, but also for the awkward situation he created when we were in his office. Whoever came in all of a sudden would not know who was who: at his request, I sat on his chair at his desk; he was standing, in front of me. He was passing sweaters and posters to me and I was signing them. They were souvenirs for his family (and he has a considerable one . . .). It was a funny situation, but also an honour. Xanana Gusmão is a great man and I was very pleased to meet him.

The visit to East Timor was about to end. But before continuing with my journey to Jakarta my presence was required at the Municipal Stadium of Dili. I was still with Xanana Gusmão when the information came that it could be a bad idea to go to the stadium, where an immense crowd was waiting for me. For security reasons my visit was not advisable, since the number of police officers was far from ideal. Here Xanana Gusmão spoke out, saying that there would be no problem, as he would accompany me to the stadium and would help protect me. "They listen to me, there is no problem," guaranteed the president of the Republic of East Timor. I was surprised and I felt special once again.

We went to the stadium. Here I witnessed something I could never imagine: more than twenty thousand people waiting for me, shouting my name. I was moved and scared at the same time. But Xanana Gusmão was true to his word: he escorted me, took charge of security and made way for me to pass, convincing the Timorese to move so that I could get onto the pitch. The police officers, led by the crowd, were even taking pictures! . . . It was difficult, but we managed to climb up to the stadium grandstand. It was incredible. Xanana Gusmão was the first to speak to the crowd. He asked for calm and pointed out the danger of a catastrophe if the crowd would not keep back, thus attempting to quieten down the euphoria. When my turn came to speak I thanked them from the bottom of my heart, for the State honours I received, the love, and the support I felt during that memorable day.

If my arrival had been complicated, the moment to leave the stadium was even more difficult. The police continued to take pictures of me and the crowd wanted to get close to me. They were climbing over each other just to get an autograph or to take a picture. My companions had to clear a path for me. It was the same scene when I arrived at the airport. People jumping over the fence, the runway invaded, a great confusion. Here the police intervened, and only then was I able to get on the plane that would take me to Jakarta.

The moments I spent in Dili were unforgettable and enchanting. I do not feel like a god, far from it, but this showed me the responsibility of being a world famous football player and the effect that someone with my media influence can have, even more so when we are dealing with a people who live in poverty like the Timorese. I shall keep the emotions I experienced in Dili well preserved in my album of memories. I feel proud for the little joy I brought to that corner of the world.

My fifth grade teacher would also be surprised if she could have witnessed that episode. Today, I cannot stop myself from smiling while recalling her concern whenever I came to class – sometimes late – with the ball in one hand.

IT WAS AN
HONOUR TO
HAVE MET
XANANA GUSMÃO

"Ronaldo, forget the ball," she would say over and over again. "The ball will not feed you. Do not miss classes. School is what really matters to you not the ball, that will not bring you anything in life." I recalled her words as I was getting on the plane. Life is full of surprises. At the time I would listen to her without paying much attention. But today I understand her and, although she keeps on saying to my mother and my aunt that she will never make this type of comment again to a student, I still think she did the right thing and that she must keep on following her belief. As a teacher, she did her job, and it was a good piece of advice, as we never know what tomorrow brings. But I never paid much attention to her.

I was a reasonable student. Of all the subjects, Science was always my favourite. Maybe it is because Madeira, my island, is volcanic and has a wide variety of plants that turn it into a magnificent garden. These classes attracted my interest and all my attention was focused on them. The Portuguese minister for Science, Technology and Higher Education, Mariano Gago, was pleased to learn about my interest. We were together at the launching of my game for mobile phones "Cristiano Ronaldo Underworld Football" – a special initiative of the Portuguese company YDreams where I have to save the football world. I heard him saying in public that I must have been "quite good" and that I was an example to children.

THE MOMENTS
I SPENT IN DILI WERE
UNFORGETTABLE
AND ENCHANTING

It was such a big honour,
to be welcomed like that,
by the Timorese people
and their President
Xanana Gusmão

YES,
IT'S REALLY ME,
AMIDST THIS
MADNESS

IF MY ARRIVAL HAD BEEN COMPLICATED, THE MOMENT TO LEAVE THE STADIUM WAS EVEN MORE DIFFICULT. THE POLICE CONTINUED TO TAKE PICTURES OF ME AND THE CROWD WANTED TO GET CLOSE TO ME. THEY WERE CLIMBING OVER EACH OTHER JUST TO GET AN AUTOGRAPH OR TO TAKE A PICTURE. MY COMPANIONS HAD TO CLEAR A PATH FOR ME. IT WAS THE SAME SCENE WHEN I ARRIVED AT THE AIRPORT. PEOPLE JUMPING OVER THE FENCE, THE RUNWAY INVADED, A GREAT CONFUSION

I am sorry I did not study more, but I had to make a choice in my life. I had just started training in the Sporting professional team, I had already been called up to play in the Lisbon team and then the national football team. To study and to play football at the same time was incompatible, and I started to slowly realise that. Following my mother's advice, I even tried to study at night. But I started to have regular training sessions with Sporting's professional squad and I would frequently arrive late at school feeling tired and worn out. I had to choose: whether I would follow a professional career as a football player or dedicate myself to studying for exams. It was not a very hard decision to make: at Sporting everything was going very well, I already trained on a daily basis with the first team and they liked me. I had hopes of becoming a professional football player some day. I left school with the support of my mother, who always encouraged me to fight for what I desired.

I did not do this without thinking, but there was a decision that I do not advise any young man or woman to make, even those who love football as much as I do. I made a mistake. Not for choosing a football career but for not appreciating my English education. "What would I want to know English for?" I kept on saying whenever I had a class. I would invariably skip it to go and play football.

When I arrived in Manchester and Alex Ferguson presented me to the squad I understood that it was a mistake. Van Nistelrooy welcomed me. "How are you?" he asked me, in a friendly way. I stood there, looking at him without knowing what to answer, as I could not understand a word he was saying. Then I remembered all the English classes I had skipped. I needed English after all . . .

MY FONDNESS FOR ADVERTISING

FOOTBALL IS MY ABSOLUTE PRIORITY, BUT I DO RECOGNISE THAT I AM VERY FOND OF ADVERTISING.

However, I do have an absolute rule, and I always stick to it: to identify myself with the product. Therefore the process of selection of endorsements is a very careful one, because this is not my main activity, as I keep on repeating. It is a consequence of my playing skills, of my standing in football, and that I represent the Portuguese national football team and, obviously, being one of Manchester United's players. And here I must mention, to be truly fair, someone that throughout my career has been the pillar of all my marketing and advertising activities: Luís Correia. He is the one who manages this process, both in product selection and the arrangement of all the details. He has always been the main force behind Gestifute, which is Jorge Mendes' company, my managing agency. He is extremely honest in what he does, is very professional, and he is also very straightforward, knowing what to do and with very precise opinions.

Filming a publicity shot, **Indonesia**

The first advertising contract I signed occurred shortly after my arrival at Manchester United and it was signed with the Portuguese financial group BES, which became my first sponsor. I was just 18 years old, with no experience, but it ended up being spectacular. The idea was also excellent: I'd shoot, shoot and shoot and the net would always swerve away from the ball, until, eventually, I'd score and the net would fall down. The recording took two days, but I never felt tired. On the contrary, I thought it was very funny, as it was my first experience in this field and it was also a very imaginative advertising concept. You can say it was almost my first experience as an actor, as I had to change my expressions depending on the shots I made . . . As the net was swerving from my shots I had to make countless expressions, from shyness, through impatience, up to the satisfaction of making the objective happen. My first experience within this field went really very well and encouraged me to have others.

One, for instance, had me inside a Coke can, doing bicycle kicks with ice cubes. That was really spectacular. That is one of the strong images resulting from my participation in the campaign promoted by Coke for World Cup 2006 and that was exclusively directed at China. The final result was really fabulous. We recorded for two days, during which I did a lot of ball juggling, sometimes wearing the Portuguese national football team shirt, and others wearing the trademark shirt of this famous cold drink, the most popular in the World. The final result was amazing, with the can coming to life and hopping as it made moves . . . with ice cubes replacing the ball.

I went to China with Manchester United during the 2005/06 pre-season – it was then that my negotiations with Coke started. I was surprised by the enthusiasm of the Chinese, they are in fact a very special people. Wherever United goes, crowds gather and everybody stops to see the team. But I was astonished at their passion for football in general and for Manchester United in particular. No one was expecting to see such a crowd at the airport to receive the team and, personally, I was caught off guard although I knew that this market was huge. With this visit I had the opportunity to develop my plan. A dribble is all that it takes to amaze these people. Now I understand this phenomenon. The passion for football makes miracles happen.

Coca-Cola®

Shooting an ad
can be very
amusing

克里斯蒂亚诺·罗那尔多

I KNEW THAT THIS MARKET WAS HUGE

Launching of the
electronic game
from YDreams

It was precisely my dedication to football that, one day, whilst still in the early stages of my career, at 11 years old, made me take the risk of playing even though I was dreadfully ill. At the time, I was playing for Nacional da Madeira and the game in question was absolutely decisive, as we needed to win in order to become champions. But I fell sick – I believe I had a fever – and nobody was counting on me any more. "I am going to play," I declared. My mother was worried and afraid. "My son, you cannot play because you are sick," she said, in an attempt to dissuade me. "Mum, I want to play. I need to play. It is a very important game. If I feel very bad and if I feel I cannot continue, I promise that I will ask to be replaced immediately," I argued. There was nothing my mother could do. Everyone was surprised to see that I was going to play. On the pitch I never even thought about the aches and pains. All I remember is that I scored a goal and we were champions. It was worth it.

I SAW ADVERTISING PEPE JEANS
AS ANOTHER PERSONAL
CHALLENGE, BECAUSE I HAD
TO POSE SIDE BY SIDE WITH A
PROFESSIONAL MODEL, USED
TO THE CAMERAS, UNLIKE ME

My first modelling experience was with the London clothing trademark Pepe Jeans and, obviously, totally different from everything I had done until then in advertising. I saw it as another personal challenge, because I had to pose side by side with a professional model, who was used to the cameras, unlike me. However, the photographer was surprised by my calmness. The location chosen was Barreiro, a Portuguese town near Lisbon and close to a factory area. It was a deserted wasteland that was ideal for the creation of some very stunning backdrops, along

MY PASSION
FOR FOOTBALL IS
OBVIOUS. I ALSO
HAVE A BOYISH
SIDE I DON'T
WANT TO LOSE
EVER

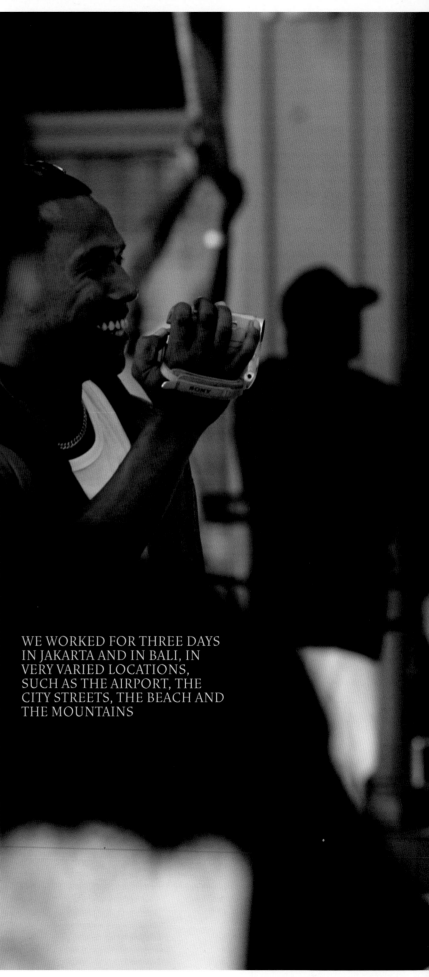

with cars and even some wolves. It was both curious and fun, although it took us two days of hard and tiring work. But it was worth it. At the end, the photographer told me that because of my calm attitude he could not believe this was my first time on a shoot.

In June 2005 I went to Indonesia to shoot an advertisement for an energy drink called Extra Joss. I regret the fact that the images have not been broadcast in Europe, because the result was incredible, but the campaign was exclusively directed to this, the greatest archipelago in the world. It was one of the most gratifying experiences I have had: for the trip, the recording concept, and the people that were with me. We worked for three days in Jakarta and in Bali, in very varied locations, such as the airport, the city streets, the beach and the mountains. I remember that the police had to close one street due to the filming.

I also recall being on the mountains and one scene, an elderly man with no shoes on, coming down from one of the hills with a basket full of coconuts on his shoulders, an image that carried me back to the 70s and to the scenes of some Vietnam War movies.

WE WORKED FOR THREE DAYS IN JAKARTA AND IN BALI, IN VERY VARIED LOCATIONS, SUCH AS THE AIRPORT, THE CITY STREETS, THE BEACH AND THE MOUNTAINS

Shooting in **Jakarta**

And . . .
action!!!

THE NATIVES
LOOKED
AT EACH OTHER,
AMAZED WITH
THE "MAGIC"
I JUST FINISHED
DOING WITH
THE BALL

The shooting in Bali started with a group of natives forming a circle, singing songs based on Hindu culture and mythology, and surrounded by fire. I was standing in the middle, barefoot, playing with the ball. When I finished my "performance", I sat on the floor, with my legs crossed, and there was an absolute silence. The natives looked at each other, amazed with the "magic" I just finished doing with the ball. The fire, the songs, the penumbra – these shootings were done just after sunset – creating an atmosphere of strong mysticism. It was both strange and spectacular. And a unique experience.

PLAYING WITH THE BALL
TO RELIEVE TENSION

I LIKE TO IMPROVISE, AS BALL DRIBBLING, POSING, SPEAKING A SENTENCE OR WHATEVER ONE HAS TO DO FLOWS MORE NATURALLY WHEN IMPROVISED. IN GENERAL, THE ONE RESPONSIBLE FOR THE FILMING OR FOR THE PHOTOS APPROVES OF THIS AND IS EVEN SURPRISED.

In my last spot for Nike – a sportswear trademark that has been part of my life from the beginning of my career – I met Eric Cantona, one of the iconic 7s of Manchester United, who hosts the show "Joga Bonito". These shoots are the easiest ones, as the ball is the great protagonist. It was done in the dressing room and in the end it was very easy. We only had to play with the ball: to balance it on our feet without letting it fall, to chest and head the ball, in short, nothing complicated. After all, these are skills I enjoy practising. This is why I am always so pleased to do the Nike campaigns.

I cannot help caressing the ball or enjoying juggling. I used to do it when I played in the street, I kept on doing it all throughout my training and I still do it now. And I will keep on doing it. This is the real Cristiano Ronaldo. I believe that when people see me on the pitch playing with the ball before the beginning of the warm-up period, they may be tempted to think that this is nothing but a charm offensive or showing off. If this is what you think then you are wrong, because I do it naturally, as you will easily understand from what I am going to say next . . .

I am one of the first, if not the very first, to arrive every day at the Manchester United training centre, and always early in the morning, because I like to do everything calmly. I have adopted a kind of ritual: I prepare myself, sometimes I eat my breakfast there, I go to the gym, once in a while I play with the ball by myself, I often do specific work to prevent injuries, exercises with chest expanders, weights, and I even play basketball with one or two team-mates who arrive meanwhile. All in the privacy of the Manchester United dressing room.

Before the matches – both for the club and the national football team – I always have the same routine. As soon as the coach reveals the composition of the team, I immediately go to the dressing room and start to juggle with the ball. We leave to warm-up and while waiting for the physical exercises to start I keep on practising my skills. I take the ball, I pass it under one foot, and then the other, I pick it up, bounce it, in short, I amuse myself with the ball. I do it just for pleasure, but there is also another reason: to put an end to any tension I may have before the match. My team-mates, in both the club and the Portuguese national team, can confirm this, as they know me very well. This is the way I have of motivating myself, of relieving the pressure of the match, of calming down, of preoccupying myself. I do not like to think much before a match and playing with the ball works as the perfect antidote, neutralising all my worries about the game. When I go onto the pitch that is time to concentrate on what is really important, but beforehand, no.

BANDA ACEH

I WAS HORRIFIED BY THE IMAGES BROADCAST OF THE TSUNAMI TRAGEDY THAT OCCURRED IN ASIA ON DECEMBER 26TH, 2004.

IN NO TIME, SEVERAL COUNTRIES IN THE INDIES WERE DEVASTATED BY GIGANTIC WAVES, CAUSING AN UNREAL SCENE OF DEVASTATION AND, EVEN MORE DRAMATIC, ALMOST 280,000 DEATHS AND MANY THOUSANDS OF PEOPLE MISSING. INDONESIA WAS THE COUNTRY THAT SUFFERED THE MOST FROM THE DISASTER.

MARTUNIS

Six months after this tragedy, I was there. To see the broadcast images or the photos is one thing, but to be there, in the middle of the ruins, the almost total destruction, is something completely different. I was impressed and moved by the scenes. But, above all, I began to deeply admire the population that, in Banda Aceh (in the north of the island of Sumatra, the one most affected), were fighting for their lives.

The Banda Aceh Mosque – the first place I visited – was almost destroyed. There was nothing left but the façade. The houses still standing could be counted on one hand. There were just piles of debris. I expected to find people terrified about what had happened, anguished, depressed, disenchanted, surrendered. But I found a people with enormous courage and determination to survive, committed to building the future and burying the past, in rebuilding their houses, because in emotional terms it is impossible for those who lived through the tsunami and everything that followed to forget. A terrible drama.

The attitude of the people of Banda Aceh after the tragedy was heroic, even though the majority had lost their families and homes. The visit to this location

was a striking moment. Still waking up from the pain, the population received me with a smile and with an extra-ordinary kindness. I thanked God for somehow being able to help them, even though only for a moment, to forget about the tragedy. I laughed with them, encouraged them, comforted them. And they paid me back with their eyes sparkling with hope for the future and they were determined to follow me to every location I was going to visit, be it on foot, bus or motorcycle. A stop had been organised at a football field, in order for me to play football with some children, but it was not possible. Leaving the bus was already complicated, because the doors would not open due to the crowd outside pressing against them. When I finally got out, the crowd was occupying the pitch, making it impossible to have any direct contact with the children.

It was also here that my second meeting took place with Martunis, a seven-year-old Indonesian boy of great courge, who survived the Tsunami all by himself, for 19 days. At the time a Sky News team rescued him he was wearing a shirt from the Portuguese national football team. The first time I had met him was in Lisbon, at a gathering of the

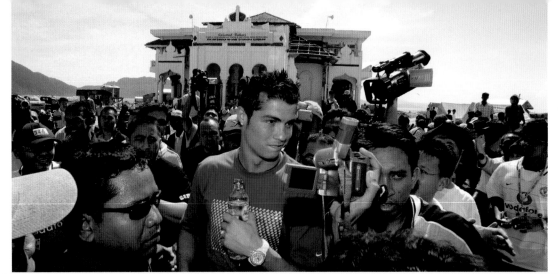

Portuguese national team, to where he and his father had been invited by the Portuguese Football Federation. He kept his shy look even when the coach, Luiz Felipe Scolari, asked him if he knew my name. He did! Later I was informed that he was a fan of Manchester United, thus explaining his prompt answer. I gave him a kiss on the forehead and promised him we would meet again.

It happened a few months later, when I visited Indonesia. We spent the day together in Banda Aceh and, once again, I was touched by his innocent look, his curiosity, surprise, and admiration, feelings that he was unable to hide. I cannot even imagine the suffering he went through during those 19 days when he wandered alone, with no news from his family, having to rely on his survival instinct. I wonder if an adult would be able to bear everything that he went through. The moment when we met again was a very pleasant one.

We talked by gestures and with the help of a translator. But he is so shy he barely said a word, he just stared. I offered him a shirt. He also received a mobile phone as a gift. He immediately asked for my number and we played with the phones right there. Side by side, we called each other and talked. That is to say, we tried. Everything was new to him. I opened my computer and his eyes opened wide, because it was the first time he had seen something of that kind. He was filled with enthusiasm when I showed him some pictures of me and some video games. His eyes were glittering

TO SEE THE BROADCAST IMAGES OR THE PHOTOS IS ONE THING, BUT TO BE THERE, IN THE MIDDLE OF THE RUINS, THE ALMOST TOTAL DESTRUCTION, IS SOMETHING COMPLETELY DIFFERENT

MARTUNIS, A SEVEN-
YEAR-OLD INDONESIAN
BOY OF GREAT COURAGE,
WHO SURVIVED THE
TSUNAMI ALL BY
HIMSELF, FOR 19 DAYS

with the sight of so many novelties in such a short time. When the local population saw that we were together, the delirium was immense. All because of him. He was the real hero and he continues to be so. He really is an example of courage. Martunis is a little boy that deserves to have everything good in his life and I am sure he is going to be a very happy child.

I said goodbye to Martunis but I did not leave Indonesia. I talked to a group of Portuguese from OIKOS [Non Governmental Organisation for Development] that was in Aceh on a humanitarian project and began to understand even better and in a more concrete way the difficulties that worried the population. Next I journeyed to Jakarta, where I was due to participate in an auction to help the Tsunami victims. Three of my shirts (two of the Portuguese national team and one Manchester United), my football boots and an autographed ball were some of the articles auctioned. I even bid for one of them and bought it in the auction, I believe for 75,000 euros, that was then given to charity. After all I had seen, it was the least I could do to try to relieve somehow the suffering of those who have been affected so much by such a cruel act of nature.

FOOTBALL: GOD'S BLESSING

I DO NOT LIKE TO THINK OF FOOTBALL AS A PROFESSION.

I WOULD NOT GO SO FAR AS TO DECLARE THAT I WOULD NOT BE ABLE TO LIVE WITHOUT A BALL BUT I CAN GUARANTEE THAT I'M NOT ABLE TO IMAGINE MY LIFE WITHOUT TRAINING, WITHOUT THE PITCH, WITHOUT THE MATCH, WITHOUT THE ENTHUSIASM OR THE THRILL OF COMPETITION.

Football is my life, my great passion, my pleasure. Many of my team-mates say that their career will end the day they wake up and feel that the enthusiasm for training has vanished, that their heart does not beat with the same intensity. I am still very young, so I cannot even think about this. Also, I look on what I do as a blessing from God. Every day we hear people complaining, saying they do not like their job, and that they only work because they need the money. In my case, I thank God for the ability to pursue the activity I love.

My mother and I, at the entrance to
Sporting's training complex, where
I had been playing for a year

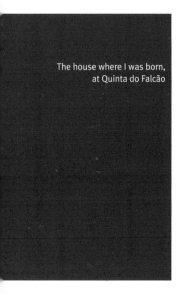

The house where I was born,
at Quinta do Falcão

The ball has always been my best friend. Apart from playing football during the school breaks, I frequently escaped from classes secretly to play with it, even when I was in the pre-primary, a convent school. The first thing I used to do as soon as I arrived home was to throw my school bag on the sofa or on my bed, to grab a banana and a yoghurt, making a hole in the top of the carton, and, with the ball under my arm I would run into the street.

Yes, I used to play in the street or, rather, in the Quinta do Falcão road, where I was born, since there was not a sports field in the neighbourhood. Me – I was then five or six years old – and my friends would use two stones to mark the width of the goal and we played right there, in the middle of the street, even though it had a steep slope. Because this was a road, we always had to watch out for the traffic. Whenever a bus came along, it had to stop a little while, wait for us to take the "goals" out of the way, and only then could it continue its journey. Then we started again: replace the stones, remove the stones. And it went on like this for five or six years, that is to say, until I left Madeira to go to Lisbon.

We used practise crosses. The ball would invariably land in my neighbours' gardens. Many of them used to complain to my mother, others would threaten to keep the ball. Some of them would keep their promises and I would go home crying. Until I learned. And everyday, Mr. Agostinho, who was very proud of his plants, would say to me: "If the ball gets in here, I will puncture it!" But I didn't take any notice, because all I wanted to do was play. I took chances and . . . inevitably, the ball would land in his garden. Every time that happened, I would run as fast as I could to get the ball out of there. He would complain to my mother, who in turn would tell me off. But the following day the very same thing would happen again. There was nothing he could do.

Whenever I wasn't playing in the street, I would go to the well, next to my house. It was a space of some 20 square metres, where I would kick the ball against the wall. I'd stay there for hours, only returning home at night, even then, only because my mother would demand my presence . . . As soon as I heard my name, I would hurry home, because there was school the next day. And if I was late, my mother would punish me: there would be no more football in the street. And that would be a real punishment to me. My mother could take away the stick or the marbles games, which I would play occasionally, but not the football.

MOMENTS CRISTIANO RONALDO

Football officially
came into my life at
Andorinha – following a suggestion from my
cousin Nuno and also because my father was
the club's equipment technician – but it was
Sporting Clube de Portugal that really launched
me. After spending two years at Nacional, the
invitation from a team on the Portuguese mainland came as something very special. At just 12
years old no one really feels the weight of responsibility, nor does one worry about the difficulties that may
arise from such a drastic change in life. It is the naivety of
children. The only thing I wanted was to play football. I could think
of nothing but that. By chance it was Sporting that was impressed by
my football – and I am glad it was, because it made my dream come true.
But I do believe that if it had been FC Porto or Benfica, my parents would
have made the very same decision: to let me go, giving me wings so that I could fly.
In other words, they understood that a great future could be waiting for me there.
I left the island of my childhood and travelled to the Portuguese mainland. I moved
to Sporting's Academy. They liked me and I became a Sporting Clube de Portugal
football player.

**THE ONLY THING I
WANTED WAS TO
PLAY FOOTBALL. I
WOULD THINK OF
NOTHING BUT THAT**

FIRST GAME
FOR SPORTING

MAIA STADIUM, 2002/03 PRE-SEASON, A FRIENDLY GAME WITH BÉTIS FROM SEVILLA. LAZLO BOLONI WAS THE COACH AT THE TIME AND HE MADE ME A PART OF THE SQUAD. I WAS ONLY 17 AND HAD MANY DREAMS.

I STARTED THE GAME SITTING ON THE SUBSTITUTES' BENCH. I WAS ALREADY THRILLED TO BE THERE, AMONGST ALL THOSE PLAYERS I ADMIRED, BUT HOPING, OF COURSE, TO BE ABLE TO MAKE MY DÉBUT WEARING SPORTING'S MAIN SHIRT. THE SCORE WAS 1–1 WHEN 20 MINUTES FROM THE END, I WAS TOLD TO TAKE THE FIELD.

The adrenalin rose. I went on and concentrated on putting into practice everything I had learned to do with the ball. I then lived one of the greatest moments of my life. With a heel kick, I placed the ball in front of me and, seeing the Bétis goalkeeper coming off his line, I aimed the ball towards the far post, using a hook shot. I was euphoric. It was not a decisive goal, it is true, but the fact that I contributed to Sporting's victory was enough to celebrate. After all, it was my début.

Finally, I managed to demonstrate all the confidence I had in myself. I still recall the day when I received the news that I was going to train for the first time with Sporting's professional squad. I spent the morning in school then, when I returned to the Academy, the B team coach at the time, Jean-Paul, wanted to talk to me. "Get ready, this afternoon you are going to train with the first team," he said. My first reaction was to run to the phone to tell my mother the news. Next, I went to the dressing room to get my football boots. I was overjoyed, but growing nervous; I counted the minutes and seconds to 4:30 pm. I still cannot describe the feeling I had when I saw the professional players arrive. I waited for the beginning of training, watching everyone and everything. I was 16 years old. I was nervous, very anxious and even afraid.

The training went on as usual but at the time I had the feeling it could have gone much better. Even so, I began to be called frequently for the professional team training. Always fearing failure and with my heart beating out of control. In those moments, I used to think: "Okay Ronaldo, you are nervous but if the coach is calling you it is because he thinks you have quality and value." This thought was always there at each training session, and it ended up being a way to overcome the fears that tormented me, even when I kept asking the same question: "What is a young boy like me doing here, amongst such great players?"

This question had a reason: when I was in the little league and a beginner, I was also a ball boy in Sporting's home matches, so I had been close to almost all those players, but on the outside. I can tell you about a curious case: Heinze, today my compatriot at United, was one of them as at the time he played for Sporting! Life is really funny: once I was Heinze's ball boy and now I play with him. We often talk about this. Beto (now a defender at the Recreativo de Huelva, in Spain), for instance, remembers me; Afonso Martins even gave me a pair of football boots . . .

FINALLY, I
MANAGED TO
DEMONSTRATE ALL
THE CONFIDENCE
I HAD IN MYSELF.
I STILL RECALL
THE DAY WHEN
I RECEIVED THE
NEWS THAT I
WAS GOING TO
TRAIN FOR THE
FIRST TIME WITH
SPORTING'S
PROFESSIONAL
SQUAD

I was ball boy for two or three years. I received five euros per game, but the money did not mean a thing when compared with the thrill of being down there, next to the pitch, close to the players and with the opportunity of being able to play with the ball during the interval. After the game, which usually took place at night, my companions and I would go to a pizza restaurant and we would party: at that time they would offer us two extra pizzas for each one we bought. We would gather all the money we had just earned, and we would buy one and go home with three. And what great sumptuous dinners we had! Two years later, I would be alongside the professional players, training with them, playing with them.

I started to be more confident as I got used to this social contact. But I felt a great conflict of emotions inside me, as I knew how much I was worth, but not able to impose myself. An anxiety forgivable in a young man with the door opened to success. It was not easy to overcome this internal struggle. Three or four months passed until I managed

Being the
youngest player
in the team, I felt
cherished by all

Laszlo Bölöni,
my first coach
as a professional
football player

to be totally calm, feeling an integral part of the team. With the work routine and the practice matches that I started playing, the pressure began to fade away, my heart beats began to be more regular and I regained my self-confidence. Even more important, I lost the fear of having possession of the ball, something I could not imagine happening until the moment I was called up to the professional squad.

During the game with Bétis, the fear disappeared. It was my second season with Sporting's first team, I was feeling more confident and integrated. I passed from anonymity to be in the newspaper headlines, which were already suggesting names of clubs interested in me. I watched this with some surprise: I thought that such a fuss was not justifiable. After all, I was just a kid and everything had been due to that game. Others followed, like the one with Inter Milan, that signalled my début in official and also European matches (Champions League preliminary rounds), or the first time I was first choice in games for the Portuguese championship. It was against Moreirense and it is

. . . THE FIRST TIME I WAS FIRST CHOICE IN GAMES FOR THE PORTUGUESE CHAMPIONSHIP. IT WAS AGAINST MOREIRENSE AND IT IS ALSO ONE MATCH I WILL NEVER FORGET. FIRSTLY, AS I SCORED TWICE, MY FIRST GOALS IN THE PROFESSIONAL TEAM

also one match I will never forget. Firstly, as I scored twice, my first goals in the professional team, and also because my mother – a real Sporting supporter from the start (as opposed to my father, a Benfica supporter) – fell ill in the Alvalade Stadium. This was caused by the emotion, the happiness, the pride of seeing her son fulfilling himself both professionally and personally.

LIVING IN THE BOARDING HOUSE AND THE DESIRE TO GIVE UP

DURING THE 2002/03 SEASON I PARTICIPATED IN 25 MATCHES AND SCORED FIVE GOALS. THE PERIOD OF MY LIFE WHEN I CONSIDERED GIVING EVERYTHING UP WAS NOW FAR AWAY, A LONG WAY FROM MY THOUGHTS.

Those were difficult moments mainly for missing my family, but also because my accent had been for a long time a target for mockery.

I was not yet 13 when I started living in Sporting's boarding house, accommodation specially designed for children coming from other parts of the country and even from abroad, who did not have any relatives in the local area. There I lived with kids of different ages, lads who were part of the beginners, youth, juvenile, or junior leagues. We were all together. Some came from Mozambique – one of Portugal's ex-colonies – and others from Monte Gordo and Lagos (in the Algarve) or from Vila Real. And there was I from Madeira. I had the typical accent of my island, noticeably different from that of other regions of Portugal. The Portuguese language is a very rich one, but just like other countries it has its different accents and characteristics. These can by themselves identify the origin of a person, whether he is from Porto or from Lisbon, if he is from the interior or the coast. But the accent from Madeira is, for those on the Portuguese mainland, difficult to understand at first . . . for those who are not from Madeira, of course!

I was short, skinny and weak. But I did it

My first day at school was terrible. I was always with Fábio Ferreira, a friend from Monte Gordo who also had an accent. It is true that one could not understand much of what he said but nevertheless we were best friends. But on that day he went to the Algarve, and I had to go to school alone, on foot, from Alvalade up to Telheiras, looking for the school. I arrived some minutes late, not many, and the teacher was already calling the roll. I was number five or six, so I raised my arm and she asked me for my name. As soon as I spoke, the kids at the back of the room started laughing and making fun of my accent. The teacher realised that I was from Madeira. But I immediately began to sweat, very nervous about the reaction of the class.

Today, I look
back and remember
with a certain
nostalgia those
difficult days . . .

The first exercises
for my first trial
practice

Today these memories make me smile. I am very proud of my accent and I find it striking. It is funny, in my day-today life I speak in a more explicit way, but when I am in Madeira or when I am in the presence of my family I change my accent completely, but in an unconscious way. To be with them is all it takes for me to speak like a real native from Madeira again. But as a child things were different. To me, it was very strange to find that no one understood what I said. There were times when I thought I spoke a different language from my colleagues and I found that very confusing. As soon as I opened my mouth, they immediately started laughing and mocking. I was traumatised. I felt like a clown. I cried with shame. I called my mother saying that I could not stand it any more, that the other kids were making fun of me, that I wanted to return home. "Go on, do not pay attention to what the others say," my mother and the rest of my family would say. They always gave me the will to continue. I did not give up, thanks to them. Eventually, I became used to those episodes and my colleagues also began to get tired, and to understand that it was not right to do all that mocking.

At the Academy I shared my room with three other kids who soon became my friends: Fábio Ferreira, José Semedo and Miguel Paixão. At the time there were not enough rooms for all, as the academy was full. I had the idea of gathering all the beds, so that we could fit in the same room. And that was what happened.

We could each phone home two or three times a week. I would run to the phone as many times as I was allowed. And I would also return to my room crying intensely and in grief. As soon as I heard the voices of my relatives I began to

miss them more. I cried almost every day. I had never felt so homesick in my life. And that was why I wanted to give up this opportunity. That situation haunted me with terrible frequency.

Here I clearly understood the price I had to pay for being away from my family and it was a real martyrdom at first. I learned how to deal with the fact that I was missing my street and Mr. Agostinho's garden. My mind was filled with so many beautiful images. I was away from my island, from my family, from my childhood friends, after all I was not growing up among those with whom I had spent my early years.

This is no job for a hero, but one can see I had to face a lot of difficulties at a very early age, along with daily responsibilities. After all, I was responsible for a series of tasks that kids do not usually have, like taking care of my own clothes, taking them to the laundry, then ironing them to present myself clean and tidy at school every day, just like my parents taught me.

With them I could be just a child, growing up without pressures or responsibilities. The first year I spent in the boarding house was very complicated. I would cry almost every day. But the same happened to my friend from the Algarve. He was even worse than me! Sometimes I would comfort him, and sometimes he would give me courage. Between 12 and 13 I was solely responsible for myself. That was when I started growing up. Inevitably such an experience helps to make any human being more mature.

AS SOON AS I HEARD THE VOICES OF MY RELATIVES I BEGAN TO MISS THEM MORE. I CRIED ALMOST EVERY DAY. I HAD NEVER FELT SO HOMESICK IN MY LIFE

. . . SPORTING
HAD REACHED
AN AGREEMENT
WITH
MANCHESTER
THAT VERY
NIGHT, THE DAY
BEFORE
THE MATCH . . .

D-DAY MATCH
WITH MANCHESTER

I ALREADY BELIEVED THAT MY LIFE WAS CHANGING AFTER MY FIRST EXPERIENCE WEARING SPORTING'S SHIRT, BUT AFTER WHAT HAPPENED ON AUGUST 6TH, 2003, MY LIFE WOULD CHANGE FOREVER.

Sporting had just built a new stadium, included in the 2004 European Championship organisation project held in Portugal. For the inauguration of the Alvalade XXI Stadium a game was scheduled between Sporting and Manchester United. On the eve of the game, my colleagues from the Academy talked only about my participation in the game. "Hey, Ronaldo, so you are going to play against Manchester! Awesome!" they would say. I smiled. "Calm down, calm down," I would reply. On the day before the match, I was filled with enthusiasm.

I played well in the match against Manchester. At the end, Alex Ferguson congratulated me and I no longer stayed in Alvalade

I managed to sleep, despite knowing that Sporting had reached an agreement with Manchester that very night, the day before the match, after a meeting held in Quinta da Marinha. This meant I already knew that United was going to be my future. Despite everything that was written at the time, Manchester's interest in me did not occur after that friendly match, so it was not even due to my performance, which I know was a good one, as I will explain. I was confident and in my head there was only room for one thought: to show them all my skills. On "M" day (for Manchester), I woke up feeling very calm, did everything as normal and waited for the start of the match.

I entered the stadium. Alvalade exhibited all its elegance and offered a fantastic environment. I was very confident and was thrilled with the reaction that came from the stands. The match began and I felt very good. So good that I believe it was my best performance ever in a Sporting shirt. In the end, I could not have been happier: my team won and everything went well. And this was not just any opponent. Manchester United has always been a great team as I knew from watching their matches on the television. I recall the pairing of York and Cole, of Cantona . . . I admired Manchester United but I had never thought that after this game my immediate destination would be that great British team. Despite signing the transfer, I thought I would be playing at Sporting for one more year.

Everything went very fast and in an unexpected way. At the end of the game, Alex Ferguson wanted to talk to me in his office. "Okay," I said. When I arrived, Jorge Mendes, my agent and also my friend, was there as well. Apart from taking care of the transfer he was also our translator. Jorge had already informed me about what was going to happen. I was thrilled, as you can imagine. The United coach, a well-known face in world football, paid me a lot of compliments that I heard through Jorge's translation. One cannot be indifferent to such compliments when coming from such a football personality. I was obviously pleased. Two days later I was in England to see the club facilities and to adjust some details of the contract.

The support and guidance of Jorge Mendes was crucial

WHEN I ARRIVED AT OLD TRAFFORD I WAS VERY NERVOUS, NOT ABOUT BEING A FOOTBALL PLAYER AT THAT MAGNIFICENT CLUB – FORTUNATELY, I HAD ALREADY OVERCOME THAT PHASE – BUT BECAUSE MY ENGLISH WAS VERY POOR.

I SIGNED THE CONTRACT, CONVINCED THAT I WOULD BE RELEASED ON LOAN TO SPORTING AND STAY THERE FOR ANOTHER YEAR. "SO, NOW YOU GO BACK TO LISBON, YOU ARE GOING TO LEARN ENGLISH AND WHEN YOU RETURN TO STAY EVERYTHING WILL BE STABILISED AND IT WILL BE GREAT," I TOLD MYSELF. ALEX FERGUSON PROBABLY GUESSED MY THOUGHTS BECAUSE HE IMMEDIATELY SAID: "WE ARE INTERESTED IN YOU, BUT FOR THIS YEAR, SO YOU ARE GOING TO STAY." I WAS SURPRISED AND A LITTLE WORRIED.

"But I came without luggage. I did not bring anything, not even clothes!" I replied. "No problem," he said. "Tomorrow you will train and then you will go to Portugal to get your things."

I was introduced to each of the players at United, I saw the stadium, the club facilities, the training ground. "Hey, I am going to play here. That is incredible!" I kept repeating to myself. I was thrilled. That feeling of being "insignificant" that I had endured when arriving at Sporting, had vanished on this journey to Manchester, I was more mature. I cannot say that I was a man at the age of 18, but I was more grown up. I was calmer, I believed in myself. In Manchester I didn't go through half of what I experienced at Sporting. I had definitely overcome my lack of confidence and my fear of failing.

I started training on the day after I arrived at Manchester. I was not a stranger, because some days previously my new colleagues had faced me as opponents – it appears that some of them had even advised on my acquisition after the game with Sporting, obviously without knowing that everything had already been arranged – and everything went smoothly.

Three days later United were playing against Bolton, and so I thought that this would be the moment for me to return to Portugal, to pack my things and finally move to Manchester. I was wrong again. "I am calling you up," Alex Ferguson said. "Already?!" I said surprised. But it was true.

Old Trafford is magnificent. I had never seen anything so impressive. The sun was shining on that magical day, the stands were filled with 70,000 fervent supporters, and there was an atmosphere both chilling and thrilling. I started the game sitting on the bench. I watched the match filled with enthusiasm, even though a little nervous. The first half ended, we all went to the dressing room to hear the coach and came back for the second half. Fifteen minutes later, Alex Ferguson turned to me and said: "Warm up." I got up and started doing some physical exercises. All the supporters applauded, as if they were welcoming me, and my heart started beating faster and faster.

VISITING OLD TRAFFORD, SIGNING AND STAYING

There were 30 minutes left to the end of the match when I heard the words; "Ronaldo, you are going on." I could not think straight. I just wanted to take my tracksuit off quickly. I was going to play in attack on the right wing. "Okay," I replied. The supporters gave a standing ovation. I was so moved and filled with enthusiasm by that whole atmosphere and the kindness shown on my début, in short, I did not want to wake up from that wonderful dream. The first time I touched the ball things went very well. I felt even more confident. I scored a penalty. The game ended but I wanted it to continue. I was considered the best player on the field and I received my first bottle of Champagne, the "trophy" that is offered in England to the man of the match. I was dreaming. At the age of 17 I had my professional début at Sporting and by the age of 18 I was transferred to Manchester United. Impossible? More than possible, it became a reality. And it all went so quickly that I almost had no time to breathe or to understand what had just happened.

I travelled to Manchester with Jorge and Luís but I was convinced I would return to Sporting

I ONLY REALIZED
THE MEANING
OF THE NUMBER 7
AFTER ALEX FERGUSON
GAVE IT TO ME

I WAS DREAMING.
AT THE AGE OF 17
I HAD MY PROFESSIONAL DÉBUT
AT SPORTING AND
BY THE AGE OF 18
I WAS TRANSFERRED
TO MANCHESTER UNITED.
IMPOSSIBLE?

OLD TRAFFORD
IS MAGNIFICENT.
I HAD NEVER SEEN
ANYTHING
SO IMPRESSIVE

TWO PLATES OF SOUP TO GROW UP

I WAS STILL A KID, BUT I WAS NO LONGER THE SKINNY CRISTIANO RONALDO, SMALL, FEEBLE, BOLD, AND WITH CROOKED TEETH, THAT HAD JUST ARRIVED AT SPORTING'S ACADEMY – ALTHOUGH I WAS BORN A REASONABLE WEIGHT, ALMOST NINE POUNDS!

MY MOTHER AND I AT CAMPO GRANDE SUBWAY STATION, THREE MONTHS AFTER ARRIVING AT LISBON. I HAD LONG HAIR BUT I WANTED TO SURPRISE HER SO I SHAVED IT

"You are a good player, but you are so thin . . ." they would say. And I was unhappy, because I knew it was true. Even when I was in the junior league, I was one of the smallest in my team. Then one day I convinced myself, encouraged by my mother, that I had to eat two plates of soup at each meal to try to improve my growth. And it really worked! Of course I do not know if it had anything to do with the soup, but the truth is that I did grow up a lot in no time and in two years I grew quite a few inches. Some people that had not seen me in a while were surprised at my growth. I was very proud of myself.

When I started playing in Sporting's first team nobody could accuse me of being small any more. I was still skinny, but I was already nearly 5 feet 10 inches tall. I was tall. And I was still fast. I stopped being the "Abelhinha" (Little Bee), the nickname I was given in the Andorinha FC for being so small, running so much, zigzagging and with small steps. It is curious to see that I still run like that. What I mean is, that now I am tall I didn't lose my speed and I continue to run with small steps. This may not be very normal, but this is the way I have always been.

THE SPEED OF FRANCIS OBIKWELU

SPEED HAS ALWAYS BEEN ONE OF MY MAIN CHARACTERISTICS. I DO NOT KNOW IF IT WAS THOSE CRAZY RUNS I DID WHEN I WAS SMALL, TO GET MY BALL BACK FROM THE NEIGHBOURS' GARDENS (IN THE STREET WHERE I STARTED DEVELOPING MY PASSION FOR FOOTBALL), OR WHEN I HAD TO RUN AWAY FROM MY SISTER CATIA WHENEVER I GOT HER MAD, THAT HAS AWOKEN THIS TENDENCY IN ME.

I always enjoyed athletics a lot. During the long period that I spent at Sporting's Academy – ever since the starters, through the juveniles up to the juniors – I rarely missed a single training session with the club athletics team. Every day I would follow the very same routine: I went to school in the morning, then after lunch I would leave the training centre, walking along a really narrow path, a short-cut to the athletics track. I would sit there, all by myself, on the stone stand and I would stay there observing the athletes training, in both speed and stamina competitions, or in the high or long jumps, or javelin. I would only return in the middle of the afternoon to train.

This was how I met Francis Obikwelu, a Nigerian athlete who became a naturalised Portuguese and who won, on behalf of my country, the gold medals in the 100m and 200m in the Gothenburg European Championships, held in 2006. I was also present at many of the training sessions of Rui Silva, one of the best middle-distance runners ever in the history of Portuguese athletics. But the speed of Obikwelu was really amazing and I was impressed by it at every training session I attended.

I was not the least surprised when he beat the European record in the 100m, running the distance in 9.86 seconds, because I knew him very well. I was thrilled when he became European champion!

"THE PORTUGUESE DO NOT MAKE THINGS EASY. THE PORTUGUESE DO NOT TAKE RISKS. THE PORTUGUESE ARE THE BEST,"

It was very funny because, at the time of the race I was with my colleagues on the Manchester United bus. We were then in the pre-season, and we were going to play our first practice match against Oxford – in which I would end up by scoring twice – and the bus television was tuned to the channel that was broadcasting the championship. Due to the different nationalities of the athletes in the race, support was divided among us. But I kept on repeating, completely euphoric: "Get ready, because Obikwelu is going to win. Obikwelu is going to win." And I would not stop saying this. And he really won! It was incredible! On that bus I was the only one to cheer. I started jumping, celebrating as if it was me who had won that race. My colleagues could not stop laughing. And when I said "The Portuguese do not make things easy, the Portuguese do not take risks, the Portuguese are the best," they looked at each other, somewhat surprised. "But he is not Portuguese . . ." they responded. "Yes he is," I guaranteed. And he is. He is a Portuguese I have known for a long time and one who fills us with pride.

I was so happy with his victory and success that, after obtaining his phone number, I sent him an SMS to congratulate him. Later I was told that he was very surprised by my message and he even commented on the fact in some interviews he gave. Great Obikwelu! He finally got the medal he wanted so much. And doubled it as well.

UP TO NOW, I HAVE HAD VERY FEW COACHES. NOT COUNTING THOSE I MET AT VARIOUS TRAINING STAGES, I HAVE IN FACT BEEN UNDER ONLY THREE: LASZLO BÖLÖNI, AT SPORTING, LUIZ FELIPE SCOLARI, WITH THE PORTUGUESE NATIONAL FOOTBALL TEAM, AND ALEX FERGUSON, AT MANCHESTER UNITED.

BÖLÖNI, SCOLARI AND FERGUSON

They are all very good coaches and they were all very important, in their different ways (as no coach is the same as another) in my development, both as a football player and as a man. I am not just saying this to be nice and friendly, believe me, as I do not need to be "politically correct" as they say. This is really what I think and the only thing I have not said yet was that I became their friend, I still am so, and I hope to continue as such.

Bölöni will always be my first point of reference because he was the one to launch me in professional football. I do not know, and nobody knows, where my career would be now if it were not for him, but the fact is that it was the Rumanian manager who appointed me to Sporting's first team when I was only 16. Bölöni was already known in France for giving young players a chance, but I must also say that Sporting has also been known for it over many years. Many other young football players succeeded in this sport that so enraptures crowds: like Paulo Futre, Luís Figo, Simão Sabrosa or Hugo Viana, just to mention a few. And also Ricardo Quaresma, in whom Bölöni invested at the same time that he did with me.

From my first training session, I saw that Bölöni had a lot of confidence in me. He would call me up from the juniors to play and he would encourage me. That was extremely important to me, as I needed to be sure that my work pleased him, thus leading me to believe that one day in the future I could be a quality football player. After this first contact with the older ones, he integrated me in the group and, little by little, he started launching me. Meaning, he did things slowly, without pressure on me, showing me that he knew what to do when working with a young football player with a great future. Such an attitude gives confidence to someone who is just starting his career.

I cannot say that I have the same close relationship with him that I have with Alex Ferguson or with Luiz Felipe Scolari. Bölöni is less

The Coach's trust is crucial for your confidence

MORAL SUPPORT IS
AS IMPORTANT AS
TECHNICAL SUPPORT

expansive and when I met him I was only 16 years old. But as a coach he helped me, for instance, to understand that in professional football there are things that we can do, but there are others we need to avoid or at least not to over-do. Believe me when I say that to have such support at that age is very important and today I do understand that very clearly. It was critical to my future.

Luiz Felipe Scolari is a very different person. He favours a closer relationship with the players, something very typical of the Brazilian people and this makes everything easier, especially with the great advantage of speaking the same language. I have an extraordinary relationship with Scolari and I can say that we are really good friends. He was the one to launch my international career. For this alone, I would consider him a very special person. But Scolari did much more than that: he advised me a lot and very well, in specific problems connected with football as well as in difficult moments that I went through in my life and that I had to overcome. I will never forget the talk we had when my father died. I was deeply touched by it. I understood that he had lived an identical experience when his father had died and we both cried.

SIR ALEX FERGUSON IS ALSO A VERY CARING COACH AND HE AND I HAVE A RELATIONSHIP THAT GOES FAR BEYOND WHAT IS USUAL BETWEEN A FOOTBALL PLAYER AND THE COACH. HE IS INCREDIBLE

But this is only one of his many features, as he is also capable of creating a great atmosphere and to joke with us. He never had to scold me and I learned a lot from him. As he had already worked with great players and shared such fantastic moments with them – namely when Brazil won the World Cup with him – he understands us like nobody else. With Scolari I am always learning. He is very special to me. I cannot stop repeating this, and I do not mean to "butter him up" as you might say, but I cannot deny the importance Scolari had to me when he picked me for the Portuguese national football team. And he is a great human being!

Sir Alex Ferguson is also a very caring coach and he and I have a relationship that goes far beyond what is usual between a football player and the coach. He is incredible. In fact, I can even say that I signed with Manchester United because of him and that it is in part due to him that I am still with the club and in England. At the end of last season, he was one of the most influential people in my decision to stay at Manchester United. After reading in the newspapers that I wanted to leave, Alex Ferguson went to the Algarve to meet me. We talked a lot, together with my agent Jorge Mendes. He told me to come back, to trust him, that things would go well and that I would have a very good reception. At that time I was convinced he wanted to help me. Fortunately I followed his advice.

Signing the renewal of the contract

At first, of course I would get a little annoyed whenever I was not a first choice. I do not like to be on the bench or not called up. I think this must be the attitude of any professional football player, for reasons of pride. But I always respected the coach's decision and today I know that his technique of launching me slowly had to do with a promise he made to Jorge Mendes, my agent. At the time, he understood that this was the most correct and reliable way for me to develop in sport and to adapt myself to a new reality. That was why – and now I do know it – Jorge Mendes chose to cooperate in my transfer to Manchester . . . That happened because it was Alex Ferguson, the coach, the person who reassured him most about the development of my career, that it would be well supported and well directed.

I remember Ferguson was the first one to support me whenever I needed a word of praise, or to solve problems. Mainly during my early times, when the adjustment to a new country and a new culture were not easy to a young man that had just arrived in a new world with such incredible prospects. I cannot forget that some years before, I was still in the street where I lived, trying to avoid sending the ball flying into the neighbours' gardens . . . In such cases, like mine, haste can be an enemy of quality. And it would have been if my development had not been very well taken care of.

BETS

ONE YEAR AFTER MY ARRIVAL AT UNITED, ALEX FERGUSON CHALLENGED ME TO A BET CONCERNING THE NUMBER OF GOALS I WOULD SCORE IN ALL MATCHES DURING THAT SEASON. THAT WAS JUST FOR FUN, BUT I BELIEVE IT WAS ALSO ANOTHER WAY OF ENCOURAGING ME.

THAT TIME, I LOST BY JUST THE SKIN OF MY TEETH: WE BET ON TEN GOALS AND I SCORED NINE!

Two years ago we repeated the challenge, but we increased the number of goals: from nine to fifteen. But, once again, I did not win. I scored twelve, being three goals away from my target. A bet is a bet, and on both occasions I tried to pay him (I do not recall the amount we agreed upon). Alex Ferguson refused to take a single penny.

As third time is supposedly lucky, at the beginning of last season we bet again. We kept the number of goals at 15, but the amounts in question were different now. Alex Ferguson proposed £100, I wanted to increase the amount and suggested £400 and he accepted. Meaning, I was the one to raise the amount, because I really believed I could do it. And I did. For the first time, I did not even had to wait for the end of the season to beat Alex Ferguson. On February 4th I scored my 15th goal of the season against Tottenham, in London. The United victory was the most important fact, but I do recognise I was more than a little pleased with myself for finally winning a bet with my great coach.

At the end of the game I was not able to talk to Alex Ferguson, as I had to join my colleagues from the Portuguese national football team – Portugal had a friendly game, in London, against Brazil. I could not do it either in the days that followed, as I fell ill with a heavy flu that gave me a fever and prevented me from getting out of the house to participate in the daily schedule of United for a few days. Approximately one week later, I returned to training and only then were we able to talk. Alex Ferguson reminded me about the bet but my answer was short and very

I DO RECOGNISE
I WAS MORE THAN A LITTLE
PLEASED WITH MYSELF
FOR FINALLY WINNING A BET
WITH MY GREAT COACH

clear: "We are even." Morally, it was not right for me to claim my prize after he had let me off the two previous years. So, I did not collect my winnings.

We did not mention the subject again. I heard him saying in an interview that he was going to double the bet and set it at 20 goals, but he has never put that proposition to me. If he had, I would have accepted of course, because I love challenges and I do think this would not be a difficult target to attain. By April I had already scored 18 goals, so . . . Next season we will see that number reached . . . ?

Alex Ferguson continues to support me a lot and I have a great respect for him. I cannot say otherwise. It would be totally unfair for me not to recognise how much I have matured as a football player (and also as a man) ever since I came to work with him.

I was only 18 when I arrived at Manchester United and I kept on improving from then on. My football ambition always had to do with imposing myself, to play at the highest level and always play well. During the first year, I was not entirely able to do it, but during my second year, from 19 till I was 20, I evolved a lot and from 20 until I was 21 the very same thing happened. I tried, year after year, to show my character, my personality, who I really am inside and outside the ground. I believe everyone now understands who Cristiano Ronaldo really is. Today I feel I have grown up a lot and I feel part of the Manchester United family, completely integrated in the group and into the club spirit, and in the city as well. I am happy. I have learned a lot from my work colleagues who not only received me very well but also protected me a lot. Everyone, from the oldest to the youngest ones in the team. Carlos Queiroz arrived at United one year after me, but he has also assumed an important role in my development. Apart from speaking the same language, I can always count on his support. He really is one of the people who have helped me a lot, who gave me a lot of strength and with whom I have a good relationship.

I SEE THAT
I REALLY AM
BETTER, BOTH
PHYSICALLY
AND TACTICALLY

I can proudly say, but without meaning to sound boastful: my progress is undeniable and is considered so by all the critics, by club colleagues, by opponents, and coaches of great experience. Probably, this is more noticeable this year, in which I am relating these events, due to the excellent success of Manchester and due to my goal scoring. But, apart from that, I see that I really am better, both physically and tactically. I have more experience, I pass the ball when I have to, I sprint in open play whenever I have the chance and I decide to strike whenever a reasonable opportunity arises. Today, I clearly have a more mature style of football, and this I also owe to the coaches with whom I worked, mainly Alex Ferguson.

My good performance during this season is mainly due to the combination of all these factors. It is obvious that the experience and maturity I acquired during the World Cup in Germany also helped. I think I matured a lot during that period, considering the pressure with which I had to deal. The World Cup helped me a lot. Here my contribution was not that good, as I am aware, but I did draw some good lessons from my participation. I learned to live with a different kind of pressure, namely that resulting from the mass media.

Looking back now, I remember I was looking forward to the beginning of the World Cup where I thought I could prove myself to everyone, because this was my first World Championship. Maybe this was not very good and ended up by lowering my confidence. But maybe it ended up as being a good thing because here I learned another lesson. The truth is that I am now much calmer, more mature and I have developed greater teamwork skills.

MY FRIEND ROONEY

AFTER THE MATCH WITH ENGLAND, I WAS CRITICISED AND WHISTLED AT. IT IS NOT VERY PLEASANT.

BUT, TO TELL THE TRUTH, IT DID ME SOME GOOD. WITH THIS I GREW WISER AND IT ENDED UP BY TURNING A PROBLEM INTO SOMETHING THAT HELPED ME TO MATURE AS A MAN AND A FOOTBALL PLAYER. WHENEVER WE GET OVERCONFIDENT WE STOP LISTENING TO CRITICISM ABOUT OURSELVES.

Today I do feel good, the team is okay and I now understand better what happened. People say we make mistakes due to our age. I do not agree. There are players of 25, 26 and even 30 who still make mistakes. This has nothing to do with age or experience. At least in what concerns me, things do not work this way. Sometimes we do things we were not supposed to do because something unexpected occurred, or because we were not prepared for a certain situation. But this can also happen to a football player in the later stages of his career. All it takes is to be distracted and not having the time to think. This can only be understood by those who are in this field, by those who are or were football players.

I progressed and matured a lot, of that I am sure. I did have some difficult moments whenever they whistled at me, but I stood up to it. I believe I did very well indeed. And I intend to go on like this, always evolving. To some people I would like only to say one thing more on this matter: I know that my friend Rooney completely understands everything I just said, even better than I. Furthermore, I insist that Rooney is a good friend, by whose side it is a pleasure and an honour to play, and he and I exchanged SMS messages just after "that" game with England, as well as the next day. We immediately cleared up everything between us, even though there was not much to be sorted. We are team-mates and we have a perfect understanding. The problem is I ended up as the scapegoat for the English defeat.

England were eliminated by Portugal, which was a situation the English did not like at all, and I was involved in it, but I was only defending my Country. They had chosen me to be the star of a movie with a totally false plot. If things were not as I have described them, then Rooney would not be my friend as he is today. I did exactly what anyone would have done.

MY FRIEND AND MANAGING AGENT, JORGE MENDES

THERE ARE MOMENTS IN LIFE WHEN WE ALL REACT ON AN IMPULSE WHEN IT WOULD BE WISER TO STOP, TAKE A BREATH AND THINK IN A MORE SENSIBLE AND RATIONAL WAY.

That is what I should have done after all that controversy concerning Rooney and me. I acted in haste when I said there were no circumstances under which I would stay at Manchester United. I said things I would not have said if I had just calmed down. Everyone makes mistakes.

The story had a happy ending. I said earlier that Alex Ferguson personally was one of the deciding reasons for me to stay at United. But there was another one, equally decisive: my agent Jorge Mendes.

I was 17 years old when I met him, but I recognised almost immediately what kind of person I had in front of me. I understood that his only goal was to support me and help me to evolve in my career. Above all, in no time I understood that he was a good man and a friend for life. So I put all my trust in him. We have now worked together for five years on a daily basis. We do not simply have a manager/football player relationship; we are good and sincere friends. Jorge is a great friend, of whom I am very fond, he is also a counsellor and, sometimes, a confidant. I trust in him with all my heart. He helped me a lot when I needed it, because there was a time when someone who could only think of his own interests was trying to exploit me and I didn't want to even waste my time with that person. Jorge appeared at the right moment to help me out of that situation. He is a friend who helps me to make long-term decisions in my life. He will always have a special place in my heart for all he means to me.

I spent part of my last summer holidays with Jorge Mendes and both our families. We have spent a lot of time together. And whenever I was not physically with him then contact would be made by telephone and that would happen almost every day. I was worried after that match with England. "Do I stay, or do I leave?" I would question myself, time and time again. Jorge gave me very serious advice at the end of the World Cup and he always emphasised his opinion: that I should stay with United. "Do things calmly. Do not rush. Manchester is the right club for you. Stay at United and then you will see if I am right or not," he would repeat almost every day.

I listened to his advice, but the final decision had to be mine. The last word was always mine, regardless of the subject in question. Later I recognised that he did give the right advice. The holidays were about to end when we had a meeting with Alex Ferguson and David Gill, president of United, in The Algarve. It was thanks to Jorge's advice that I ended up deciding to stay at Manchester United. It was undoubtedly the right decision. And now we have the confirmation.

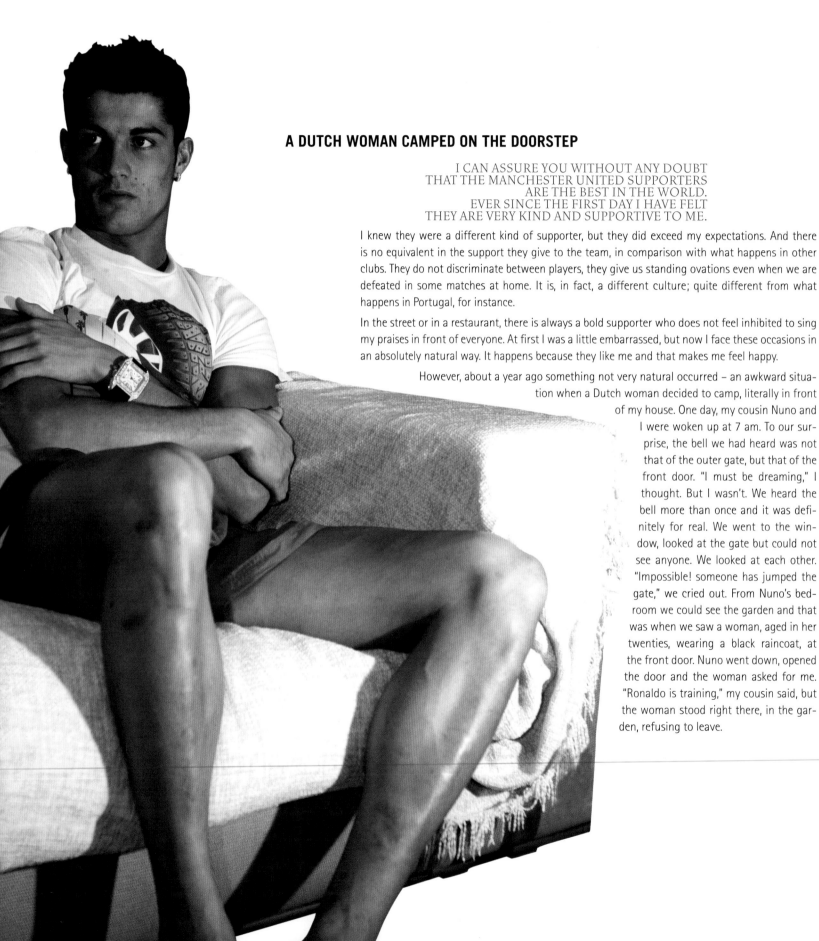

A DUTCH WOMAN CAMPED ON THE DOORSTEP

*I CAN ASSURE YOU WITHOUT ANY DOUBT
THAT THE MANCHESTER UNITED SUPPORTERS
ARE THE BEST IN THE WORLD.
EVER SINCE THE FIRST DAY I HAVE FELT
THEY ARE VERY KIND AND SUPPORTIVE TO ME.*

I knew they were a different kind of supporter, but they did exceed my expectations. And there is no equivalent in the support they give to the team, in comparison with what happens in other clubs. They do not discriminate between players, they give us standing ovations even when we are defeated in some matches at home. It is, in fact, a different culture; quite different from what happens in Portugal, for instance.

In the street or in a restaurant, there is always a bold supporter who does not feel inhibited to sing my praises in front of everyone. At first I was a little embarrassed, but now I face these occasions in an absolutely natural way. It happens because they like me and that makes me feel happy.

However, about a year ago something not very natural occurred – an awkward situation when a Dutch woman decided to camp, literally in front of my house. One day, my cousin Nuno and I were woken up at 7 am. To our surprise, the bell we had heard was not that of the outer gate, but that of the front door. "I must be dreaming," I thought. But I wasn't. We heard the bell more than once and it was definitely for real. We went to the window, looked at the gate but could not see anyone. We looked at each other. "Impossible! someone has jumped the gate," we cried out. From Nuno's bedroom we could see the garden and that was when we saw a woman, aged in her twenties, wearing a black raincoat, at the front door. Nuno went down, opened the door and the woman asked for me. "Ronaldo is training," my cousin said, but the woman stood right there, in the garden, refusing to leave.

As Nuno's English is basic, we decided to call, with the utmost urgency, our friend Rogério who has lived in England for some years. Half an hour later, Rogério arrived, and tried to get rid of her: "Ronaldo is training, he will not come back for a while, so you had better leave. It is no good staying here, in the cold and rain." Then he put her in his car to take her to a hotel, persuading her to leave the house with the promise that he would take me there in the afternoon.

Obviously I never went to meet that lady in the hotel. I did not know what her intentions were! In view of what she had done, this was all very strange. I went training, returned home and we were just preparing to leave when we saw the very same woman close to the gate. I was not sure what to do, but Rogério felt I ought to say "hello". Then she told me a great story – that I had been in Holland and had looked at her in a very special way . . . and she had saved herself for me. I did not know whether to laugh or cry. I was sure I had never seen her before in my life. But she would not go away from my door.

This story became a lot more fantastic than that. We heard she had already been at my house the day before. A neighbour, thinking that this was a strange occurrence, had talked to her and heard the same story she later told me. She came from Holland just to meet me, she had no money and no place to stay. My neighbour had taken her to a boarding house and left her there. But she did not give up. After a lot of talking, Rogério managed to get her mother's telephone number and I made the call. Her mother confirmed that she came to Manchester just to see me. "I can not believe this, it is crazy," I said.

I gave Rogério £200 and asked him to take her to the airport, buy her a plane ticket to return to Holland then make sure she got on the plane. "Okay, everything is solved," Rogério confirmed. This was a relief, but not for very long. Less than a month later, my cousin was just leaving the house and was faced with . . . the Dutch girl. "Hey?!" Nuno exclaimed when he saw her sitting at the door waiting for us. She had jumped the outer gate again, had entered the garden and camped right in front of the house. Rogério again took her to a hotel, but she returned at exactly the moment when we were leaving the house. There was a taxi parked in the street and, all of a sudden the door opened and we heard an already familiar feminine voice saying: "Surprise!" By this time I was running out of patience. We threatened to call the police, telling her that it was no use persisting because she would not get anything from me. She seemed to be convinced because she never came back again, happily for both her and us.

ASKED HIM TO TAKE HER TO THE AIRPORT, BUY HER A PLANE TICKET TO RETURN TO HOLLAND THEN MAKE SURE SHE GOT ON THE PLANE

THOUSANDS OF LETTERS ANSWERED

MANCHESTER UNITED RECEIVES THOUSANDS OF LETTERS ADDRESSED TO ME. AT A CERTAIN POINT I DECIDED THAT IT SHOULD BE ME THAT SHOULD TAKE CARE OF ALL THAT MAIL INSTEAD LEAVING IT TO THE CLUB.

At home I have one or two awards as best player resulting from a vote among the supporters. I feel I have the moral obligation to thank them. So to do this I now answer all these letters sent to me. I receive all kinds of requests, from autographs, to photos, shirts, birthday cards, or even money, believe it or not. Inside one of the countless boxes where that huge amount of correspondence is stored, a while ago I found a request for the financing of a snail breeding nursery. Someone else wished to decorate their living room with a certain painting and considered the possibility of asking me to pay for this pretension and even sent me her bank account number, and this item is not even the most striking one. People ask me for all kinds of things and they enclose bank statements, account numbers, copies of tax details with respective identification number, and even identity cards. Some go even further and send me copies of their mortgage and/or monthly car payments.

But I also receive presents from some fans who want to be different and from others who do have some sense of humour. I have already been sent caricatures, almost all of them drawn by children, albums with photos or even paintings of me. However, there is a certain Portuguese emigrant, settled in France, that deserves a special mention for the originality of his initiative. This Portuguese man sent me a shirt from the Portuguese national football team and, unlike my initial assumption, the idea was not to have me autograph it and to send it back to him but it was really a birthday gift to me and I received it in January of this year. "I imagine everyone asks you for shirts with your name and autograph on it, but I'm sending you a Portuguese national team shirt with my name on it with a number of my own choice. Just to be different," he explained in the letter he sent me. I thought it was great. The shirt, which is now in my house in Manchester, has the number 28 on it and the name S. Ferreira on the back which, going by the content of the letter must be the name of this Portuguese emigrant. I thought it was so funny that, without being asked, I sent him a note of thanks as well as my autograph, which I took great pleasure in signing.

I RESERVE ONE DAY PER WEEK TO TAKE CARE OF CORRESPONDENCE, WHICH ARRIVES FROM ALL OVER THE WORLD

I reserve one day per week to take care of correspondence, which arrives from all over the World. Some people send me self-addressed and stamped envelopes, but this does not happen with all of them. For instance, in one month I have spent more than two thousand pounds on envelopes and stamps! I sign all the letters, one by one, in my own handwriting. It may be tiring, but this is a way I can repay the supporters for all their support and adoration. My cousin Nuno and my friend Rogério open the letters, get everything ready and then I sign. To answer the fans is one of my priorities, it is something I want to do. I have that obligation and will keep on doing it. I feel even more motivated and proud.

Something identical happens with the requests for shirts. I have never charged one penny for a shirt I have offered and I've lost count of how many I have already given away. And I buy them myself. It is obvious I cannot comply with all the requests, particularly the more extravagant ones. As I used to say, the man that pleased everyone was born and died on the very same day. Not even God, and certainly even less, Cristiano Ronaldo. Here common sense must rule.

Meeting the kids in **Dubai**

IT DOESN'T TAKE A LOT TO MAKE OTHERS HAPPY

I LIKE TO MAKE OTHER PEOPLE HAPPY. IN THE VERY SAME WAY I FEEL THAT I HAVE THE DUTY OF ANSWERING, IN MY OWN HANDWRITING, THE LETTERS THAT ARE SENT TO ME BY THE SUPPORTERS, I ALSO CONSIDER THAT IT DOES NOT TAKE MUCH TO GRANT SOME MOMENTS OF HAPPINESS TO THOSE ON WHOM LIFE HAS PLAYED SOME TRICKS.

This is why I participate, whenever I can, in charity events. Not out of obligation, but because I want to and I think I should have that social and moral attitude.

Why not offer one day that is different and happy to those who need something good in their life? At least, I try to relieve them of some suffering they may be going through. I think that all those receiving adoration from the public should act like this. It is a pay back. It is a way of showing love to our neighbours, to help them believe that they can solve their own problems, that they can overcome their difficulties, no matter how bad they may seem. I feel this need to make others happy, by signing autographs, giving a photo, returning a friendly word.

As long as I have some time available, I do not refuse an autograph, no matter under what circumstances, although I do have a trick. When I am surrounded by lots of people I use the initials, CR7 and when there are fewer requests I do my regular signature, but I never complain about it. Sometimes our presence is all it takes to give someone hope. The sick children and the orphans, as well as the elderly particularly concern me. It worries me that people are dying from hunger. That is why I engage myself, whenever I can, in charity events.

During the Christmas holidays Manchester United organises visits to hospitals, so that children can enjoy something different. We bring them presents, we talk to them, play with them, bring some joy into their lives. We are also filled with the emotion of those moments. It is so easy for us to contribute to these small/big moments . . .

Some time ago, a little girl of 12 or 13 visited Manchester United. She had cancer and knew she was going to die. But she wanted to meet the players. Me included. When Bart (a United director) introduced me I was unable to ignore that sparkle in her eyes. She gave me her hand. I kissed her on the cheek and gave her a big strong hug. She knew what was going to happen to her, but at that moment she was happy, as she had been able to make one of her dreams come true. And she kept on smiling. These are the things that affect me the most, leaving deep scars in me. I said goodbye to her with a broken heart, but returned her happy smile. Sometime later, I was turning over the pages of the club magazine and I stopped at one particular page. "In memory of . . ." I had just found the news of the little girl's death. My eyes filled with tears. Life can be so unfair, I thought. Unfortunately, these cases continue to happen and I have already dealt with two or three other identical cases. These are traumatic experiences, but at the same time comforting ones because we know we ended up doing some good to someone who was ill and had a short life expectancy. And it comforts us somehow. Not for very long, because it is sad to be in the presence of someone that knows they are going to die.

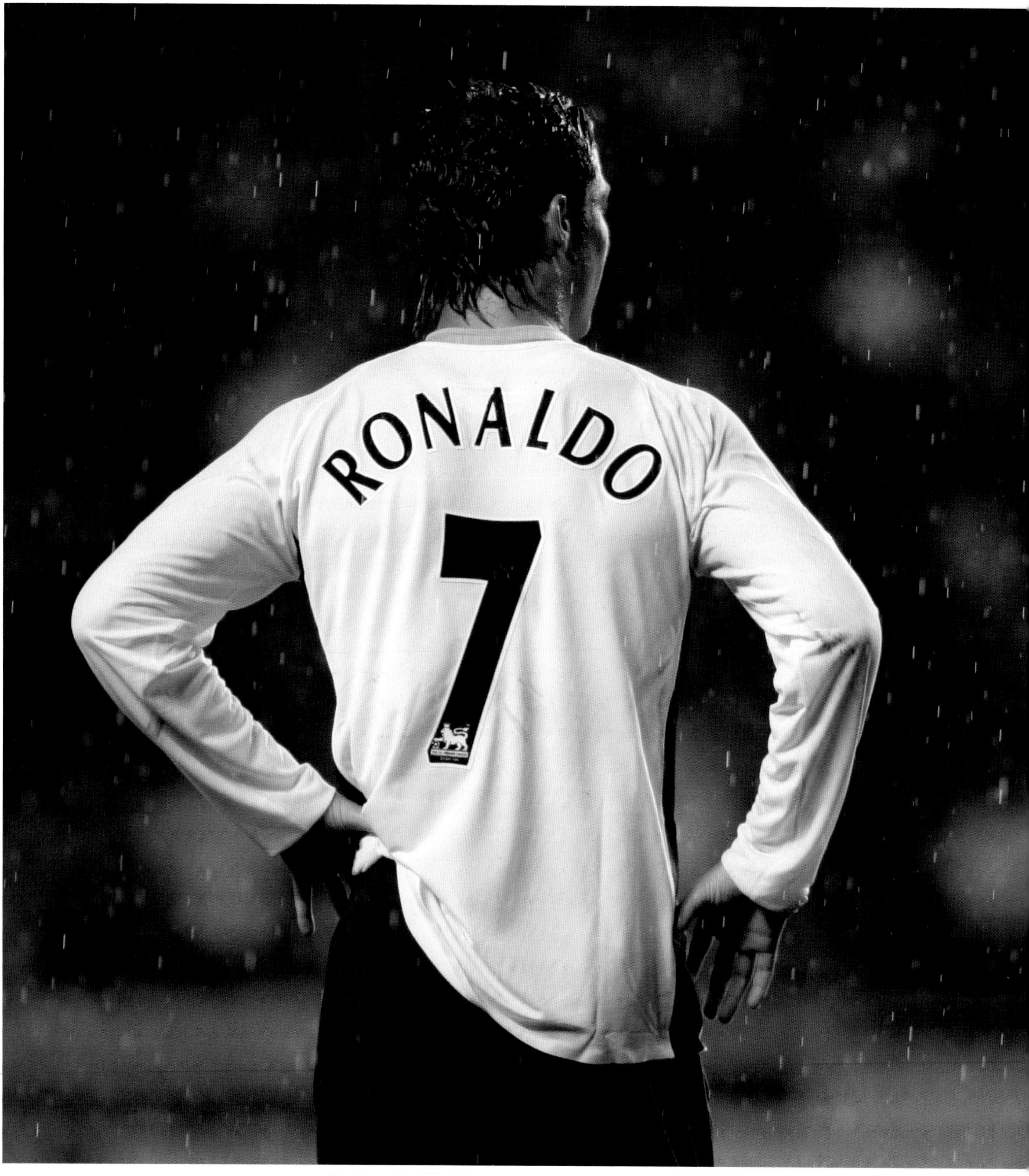
RONALDO
7

No.7, AN ICONIC SHIRT

I ALWAYS LIKED THE NUMBER SEVEN, BUT IT WAS NOT MY FAVOURITE. WHEN I WAS IN THE JUNIOR RANKS OF SPORTING I WORE IT IN MATCHES, BUT AFTER BEING CALLED UP TO THE PROFESSIONAL SQUAD THE NUMBER 28 SHIRT BEGAN TO HAVE MORE MEANING FOR ME.

That was the one I used in all the matches, and I lived the best moments at Sporting wearing it. When I was going to sign the contract with Manchester United, Alex Ferguson asked what number would I like to have on my shirt. "28," I replied without blinking, especially because I saw nobody else was using it. "No," responded Ferguson. "You are going to have number seven." I did not contradict him. "Okay," I said.

The number 7 is a mythical number for Manchester United, for the supporters, for those who have been there and to all those who are well acquainted with the history of English football and this great club in particular. Today it is my number and I am very proud to wear it. At the time, and with all the excitement of the moment, I did not even think of George Best, Bryan Robson, Eric Cantona or David Beckham, sacred names in the history of United. It was only afterwards that I stopped to think. "Wait a minute, the shirt with number 7 has an incalculable value to the club." After that I realised that by giving me this number they were also giving me a great responsibility. I was forced to live up to such an honour. To wear the United shirt was important enough; to wear number 7 as well became an extra factor of motivation.

It did not diminish nor has it increased my ambition. I felt that I had to honour that shirt. I believe I am doing it and that I will not let my coach down. This is in fact an iconic, historic number with an enormous importance. It is an honour to have it on my shirt. I would never go back, but if I had kept the number 28 who knows if it could not have become historic as well? Of course I am joking . . .

7.
NEW WONDERS
OF THE WORLD

**I READ THAT NUMBER 7,
AMONG OTHER MEANINGS,
REPRESENTS "THE SYMBOL
OF PERFECT TOTALITY".**

I DO NOT PRESUME TO INCLUDE MYSELF
IN THAT DEFINITION. I REFER TO IT
JUST TO MENTION THE SELECTION
OF THE 7 NEW WONDERS OF THE WORLD,
AND THOSE CAN BE DESCRIBED
AS A PERFECT GROUP.

I bring up this subject because I had the privilege of being invited to be an "international ambassador of this world-wide initiative on behalf of the protection of artistic and architectural works of civilisation". The event organisers argued that I was one of the "World's sporting wonders". I cannot thank them enough. I naturally accepted it with pleasure and pride.

The Acropolis (Greece), Alhambra (Granada), Angkor (Cambodia), Chichén Itzá (Mexico), Christ Redeemer (Brazil), the Roman Colosseum (Italy), Statues of Easter Island (Chile), the Eiffel Tower (France), the Great Wall of China (China), the Hagia Sophia (Turkey), Kiyomizu Temple (Japan), the Kremlin and Red Square (Russia), Machu Picchu (Peru), Neuschwanstein Castle (Germany), Petra (Jordan), the Pyramids of Giza (Egypt), the Statue of Liberty (USA), Stonehenge (United Kingdom), Sidney Opera House (Australia), the Taj Mahal (India) and Timbuktu (Mali) represent the 21 works

to be voted on, in an initiative of "The New 7 Wonders of the World". These were the architectural works scrutinised, in the first phase, among hundreds of other proposals and, in the second phase, among 77. As far as I know, this is the largest vote ever held on a global scale.

Besides, it is a project where, for the first time, all humanity can participate, as it involves all continents and cultures. And it will be immortalised in world history as the moment when, in a direct way, more than 3,691,984,877 people have united themselves around a single purpose: to turn the Planet Earth into a place more pacific, beautiful and with more history to be told in the future.

The selection of Portugal as the stage for the final announcement of this important and historic event was disclosed on September the 5th 2007, in Athens, in the "World Tour" start – a launch campaign that covered all the candidate monuments and that has counted on the presence of the most distinguished State figures of each country.

Once again, I thank the organisers for the honour of choosing me as an international ambassador.

I HAD THE PRIVILEGE OF BEING INVITED TO BE THE INTERNATIONAL AMBASSADOR OF THIS PLANETARY INITIATIVE

7, THE POOL OF THE NEW HOUSE

EVER SINCE I WAS A BOY, I HAD A DREAM: TO BUILD A LARGE HOUSE, FOR ME, FOR MY FAMILY AND ALSO FOR MY FRIENDS, A SPACE THAT IS NOT JUST A HOUSE, BUT RATHER A HOME, WHERE I CAN FEEL REALLY COMFORTABLE. THAT WISH IS NO LONGER UTOPIAN. I AM GOING TO OWN THE HOUSE OF MY DREAMS. A LARGE FAMILY HOUSE, WITH EVERYTHING I HAVE ALWAYS HOPED FOR.

I talked to Jorge Mendes about this project of mine. His immediate reaction was to suggest the name of an architect, Eduardo Souto Moura, the designer, among many other works, of the Braga Municipal Stadium. António Salvador, the president of Sporting de Braga, with whom I get along very well, also told me that Moura was the ideal person to make my wish come true. And so it was.

Our first contact was enough to establish a strong bond. I was charmed by his simplicity and humble demeanour. And he surprised me when, at the end of dinner, he grabbed a napkin and, right there, he drew the sketch of my project. I had found the person who was to be responsible for the design of my house.

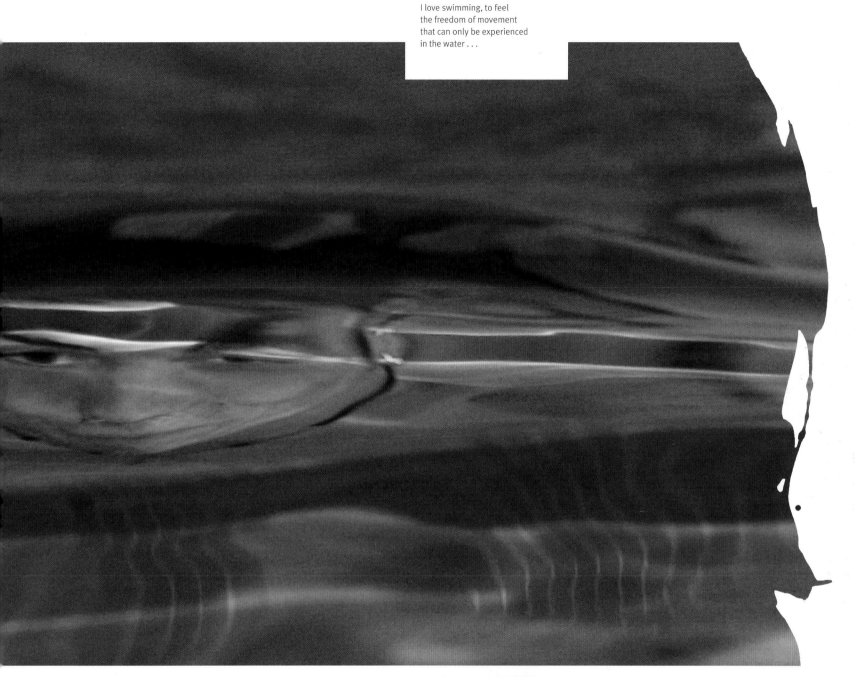

I love swimming, to feel
the freedom of movement
that can only be experienced
in the water . . .

As usually happens with all homes, mine will be quite personalised. I will not disclose too many details, as everyone knows how much I value my privacy. However, I can reveal that the number 7 will play a prominent role in it. This will happen in two ways. My house will have seven rooms, and the swimming pool will be built in the shape of a 7, a specific request of mine, which architect Souto Moura conceived in an absolutely remarkable manner.

The final review of the project for the new house, with architect Souto Moura

WHAT IS THE USE
OF POSSESSING A
COMFORTABLE
BANK ACCOUNT,
IF WE CANNOT
ENJOY LIFE PROPERLY?

7, A PROJECT FOR THE FUTURE

THIS NEW HOUSE WILL BE THE LARGEST INVESTMENT I HAVE MADE UP TO NOW. IT IS TOTALLY JUSTIFIED, AS IT IS THE FULFILMENT OF A DREAM.

I DO NOT LIKE BEING A SLAVE TO MONEY. THIS MEANS THAT IN THE DISTANT FUTURE, WHEN MY CAREER AS A PROFESSIONAL FOOTBALL PLAYER ENDS, I WILL TRY TO LIVE OFF THE INVESTMENTS I MAKE THROUGHOUT THE YEARS, BUT NOT LIVE FOR THE SAKE OF THOSE INVESTMENTS.

What is the use of possessing a comfortable bank account, if we cannot enjoy life properly? I am 22 years old, and I believe I have enjoyed life much more than my mother, who is 52 . . . Obviously, I am aware of the need to provide for the future, but I do not allow myself to become a hostage to material possessions. I believe I will maintain precisely the same ideas a few years from today.

I am satisfied with the money I have been earning, and until now I must say I cannot complain, since I have no financial problems – myself of course, nor my family. Likewise, I did not complain when I received a 50 euros monthly allowance from Sporting, when I played in the training division and lived in the training camp. During the first years of my career, I decided that my mother was the right person to manage my money. Therefore, every cent I received did not touch my hand; it went straight to her. Only later would my mother send me the amount she considered enough for me to buy the few things I needed, which were basically toiletries and clothes. When I earned 50 euros, she would send me 25. When I signed my first contract with the senior team – a little better – I earned 250 euros, of which 50 euros were for me and the rest was managed by my mother, who set this remainder aside, as if it were a fund. My sisters and my father sometimes sent me small amounts of money, which they spared with much difficulty. That is also the reason why, today, I help them with everything they need. If we do not help our family, who are we going to help?

MY BIGGEST EXTRAVAGANCE AT THE TIME, WAS BUYING MY FIRST CAR, WHICH I STILL OWN . . .

This was a method of acquiring self-discipline and controlling expenses. I knew that if I kept all the money I earned, I would always be tempted to spend it. That is why I never wanted to live wildly, and preferred to keep only the amount of money I needed to cover small expenses. Also I knew that as long as the money was managed by my mother, it was in very good hands. The same thing happened when I began to earn wages of more than 600 euros, at the time I left the Sporting training centre – where I spent five years – and went to live, along with a friend, in a boarding house in Marquês de Pombal Square, in the centre of Lisbon.

My biggest extravagance, at the time, was buying my first car – a Mercedes 220 CDi – which I still own, although it is in Madeira. As soon as I was 18 years old, I took my driving test, and the bus was replaced by the car. I lived in the boarding house for a year, and after that I moved to Manchester.

I am not obsessed with clothing, although I like to be aware of what goes on in the world of fashion. Some friends, as a joke, suggested that I should try the catwalk when my career in football ends. Quite honestly, I do not foresee that. I intend to play until after I am 30 years old, as long as possible, preferably keeping up my present level of performance. If that happens, then I will feel extremely proud of my career. Obviously, right now I do not even think about it, for I am still very young. Only when I reach that age will I be able to evaluate my physical condition, and discover what my frame of mind will be. But stepping from the football pitch to the catwalk, that cannot be. How on earth does a fashion model start a career in his thirties?

When I reach my thirties, maybe even closer to being 40, I would like to build a hotel: a resort, preferably in Madeira, where people could spend beautiful, pleasant and peaceful moments. A seven star hotel – I believe that at the moment there is only one of those in Europe. It would be called CR7, of course. After all, this is the number of my life.

This project may even be a pipe-dream, but I still have a lot of time ahead of me before I begin thinking about it. And that will only happen after my career ends. Not before that. Because my one concern is, and will continue to be, to play football. And only that.

I INTEND TO PLAY
UNTIL AFTER
I AM 30 YEARS OLD,
AS LONG
AS POSSIBLE,
PREFERABLY
KEEPING UP MY
PRESENT LEVEL
OF PERFORMANCE.
IF THAT HAPPENS,
THEN I WILL FEEL
EXTREMELY
PROUD OF
MY CAREER

HIS MAMA'S BOY

MY FAMILY MEANS EVERYTHING TO ME. THOSE WHO KNOW ME WELL, KNOW THAT I LIVE SURROUNDED BY MY MOTHER (MARIA DOLORES), MY SIBLINGS (HUGO, CÁTIA AND ELMA), MY BROTHER-IN-LAW ZÉ (JOSÉ PEREIRA), AND MY COUSIN NUNO VIVEIROS.

At my sister Elma's wedding

It has been like this ever since I was very young. I was only truly alone when I went to Sporting.

I learned to love my family, and I have already told them how hard it was being away from them in those first years, living in Sporting's boarding house. It was difficult. Maybe that is why I have grown even fonder of my family than when I was a boy.

My mother, well!, she is my mother, and we have a very special relationship. I have always been her little boy, and even today she still treats me as if I were a baby, or a small boy of five, six, or seven years old. Our relationship is fantastic. For all that she taught me, for her constant concern with my protection, for the support she has always given me. She has never abandoned me, even when we had to separate when I joined the Sporting Academy. Due to life's circumstances, my mother could only be in Lisbon three times a year. That was all she could do, but she always held my hand, and more than that, held me in her arms. She gave me support, and a powerful incentive. She is also a friend to whom I often turn to ask for her opinion about almost anything because I believe that my mother, above all people, has the right to express her opinions and tell me anything she feels like saying. So I listen to her, for I consider her the right person to give me advice and to tell me what I should or should not do in my life, whatever the subject under discussion.

My most fervent wish is that she enjoys good health and that she is happy. Because I love my mother.

I worry about her, when emotion overtakes her and she ends up feeling unwell during some of the matches that she watches. The first time it happened was in my debut at Sporting, as I told you before. I found out afterwards, that when I scored the first goal she had to have medical assistance inside the stadium, due to the excitement, and it happened again when I scored the second goal.

It was even more serious when she passed out during the Portugal–England match, in Euro 2004. Luckily, she recovered shortly after, but she did not watch the last part of the game. To prevent further upset, now she does not watch any penalties I take. She watches the games – does not miss one – but at the moment of the penalty she gets up and disappears, then returns a little later. When she watches the games on television, she only watches the replays. I also think it is better this way. Even though, luckily for me, I have not missed many.

I have a great relationship with my three siblings, whom I consider fantastic. But when I was small, I used to play more with Cátia, who is closer to my age; we played typical sibling pranks, mixed with fights. I teased her in front of my friends. She got mad at me, I ran away, she told my mother, and this went on and on.

With Hugo, the eldest of the four of us, I played football, while Elma was the quiet one, but at the same time the most balanced, the one who gave me more advice. She may not talk too much, but when she does talk, she says very wise things.

FAMILY AND FRIENDS
ARE ALWAYS
A PART OF MY LIFE

I HAVE A SPECIAL RELATIONSHIP WITH MY MOTHER. I WAS ALWAYS HER BOY AND SHE KEEPS TREATING ME AS A BOY. SHE IS A FRIEND I TURN TO A LOT BECAUSE MY MOTHER, MORE THAN ANY ONE ELSE IN THE WORLD HAS THE RIGHT TO SPEAK HER MIND AND TELL ME WHATEVER SHE FEELS

SANTA RONALDO CLAUS

MY NEPHEW RODRIGO (SIX YEARS OLD), AND NIECES LEONOR (TWO YEARS OLD) AND BEATRIZ (SEVEN YEARS OLD) ARE THE JOY OF THE FAMILY. UNFORTUNATELY, I CAN ONLY BE WITH THEM IN THE SUMMER, AND IN WINTER, WHEN I AM ON VACATION, AND IN THE CHRISTMAS SEASON. THEY SURPRISE ME EVERY MOMENT WE SPEND TOGETHER, FOR THEY HAVE ALWAYS LEARNED A NEW WORD, OR A NEW TRICK THEY HAD NOT SHOWED ME, ANOTHER PRANK PREPARED. CHRISTMAS TIME IS WHEN WE HAVE THE MOST FUN, WHEN WE GET TOGETHER IN MANCHESTER. UNLIKE WHAT HAPPENS IN OTHER COUNTRIES' LEAGUES, THE HECTIC CALENDAR OF ENGLISH FOOTBALL DOES NOT ALLOW FOR LONG BREAKS, SO MY FAMILY HAS TO COME AND VISIT ME. I HAVE BEEN LIVING IN MANCHESTER FOR FOUR YEARS NOW, AND ONLY ONCE HAVE WE FAILED TO MEET, BECAUSE IT WAS UTTERLY IMPOSSIBLE. ALL OTHER YEARS THEY CAME TO BE NEAR ME, KEEPING ME WARM IN THIS BEAUTIFUL SEASON.

Tradition is the rule, and even Santa Claus is obliged to stop at my house on the night of 24th of December. I believed in Santa Claus until I was quite grown up. I was around 10 or 11 years old when I found out that the mythical figure does not ride a reindeer, nor has a long fluffy white beard. But until that discovery – I cannot explain how it happened – my childish imagination was fired with the arrival of the Christmas season.

I wrote a list of the presents I wanted to get, and I waited for Christmas Day. Santa Claus was always very kind to me. But to tell the truth, I never asked for anything extraordinary, nor was I too demanding about the presents I asked Baby Jesus for. My biggest extravagance was a bicycle, which I got, and I cherish that memory as one of the best gifts I ever received.

In Madeira, the tradition is to open the presents only on the morning of the 25th, and that was how it always was at our house. After dinner, on the 24th, my family went to the Midnight Christmas Mass, and my mother made me go to bed very early, or else Santa Claus would not stop at our door. So I finished dinner and went immediately to bed expectantly, wanting only to fall asleep as quickly as possible, then to wake up early the next day and run towards the Christmas tree.

These memories are still very vivid for me, and that is precisely why I make an effort to pass on to my nephew and nieces the same excitement I felt about Christmas time. There is nothing like the happiness of a child. For this reason, year after year, I have been feeding all their fantasies, embodying the cheerful figure of Santa Claus.

A little while before midnight, on the evening of the 24th, I sneak out of the room, I go up to my bedroom, stuff a few pillows around my abdomen to get that "belly", I put on the red suit and the huge white beard, then I throw the sack with the presents over my shoulder and leave the house furtively. I yell "Ho, ho, ho, ho," trying to give my voice a deep tone. I ring the doorbell countless times and I carry on: "Ho, ho, ho, ho, are there any kids in this house?" It is incredible. They get over-excited, joyful as only children can be. But they are growing up and they are smart kids. They have already begun to suspect that Santa Claus looks somewhat like their uncle. I did not want their fantasy to end too soon, so last Christmas we decided to switch characters, and my friend Rogério started to play this role. He played it perfectly, and he even improvised, entering the house through the window, instead of ringing the doorbell. It was the first time I did not pretend to be Santa Claus. But this was the formula we came up with to keep Rodrigo, Leonor and Beatriz believing.

I HOPE THAT
RODRIGO,
BEATRIZ AND
LEONOR WILL
KEEP ON
DREAMING

I LOVED AND STILL LOVE MY FATHER, DINIS AVEIRO, VERY MUCH. UNFORTUNATELY, I CANNOT ENJOY HIS PHYSICAL PRESENCE ANY MORE, BUT I ALWAYS FEEL HIM CLOSE TO ME.

HE IS ALIVE IN MY MIND, WHATEVER I DO, WHEREVER I AM. I KEEP MANY FOND MEMORIES OF HIM, BECAUSE HE WAS FUNDAMENTAL TO MY DEVELOPMENT AS A FOOTBALL PLAYER, AS A PERSON, AS A MAN. HE WAS TRULY ONE OF THE PEOPLE RESPONSIBLE FOR WHAT I AM TODAY.

MY FATHER'S DEATH

The pride he had in me was all too evident and obvious, even when I first started to kick the ball in Andorinha, where he worked as an equipment technician. Not a day went by when he did not tell everyone, in detail, everything I had done, in every game. Whenever I scored a goal, I knew that when I arrived home I would have a surprise waiting for me: he brought me candy, cakes, many sweet treats, we had a great family celebration.

My father and I were always very close. He watched my training sessions, gave me advice, and we had lunches together. This was a daily routine. When he realised everyone around him was praising me, he would not utter a word, completely delighted, excited, and very proud. But if anyone dared to make a less positive comment about me, he would argue strongly in my defence. His friends, who knew him well, would take the opportunity of a not-so-good game to tease him. Obviously, he reacted: he argued, he got mad, and he never allowed anyone to criticise me. If I gave a good performance in the next game, or scored a goal, he went there the next day with a huge pile of newspapers in his hands, which he had bought very early in the morning, to give one to each of his friends, like a small revenge, but without malice. He would never shut up, whatever the circumstances. Watching me play was his passion, and he felt deeply joyful for sharing my passion for football.

Andorinha was one of the weakest teams in the championship, and when we played against stronger clubs, like Marítimo, Machico or Câmara de Lobos, defeat was invariably certain and by many goals. I remember one time that I decided I did not want to play in a certain game because I already knew we were going to lose, probably some 15-0. "What am I going to do there?" I thought. When my father found out I was not in the dressing room, he did not hesitate. He headed home, talked to me, explaining that only the weak give up. And so he encouraged me, took me to the ground and I did play. We were thrashed, of course, but I was infected with my father's enthusiasm. He was ultimately one of the people responsible for my not giving up football. My mother, who was also passionate about football, repeatedly insisted to my father that he should take me to the club where he worked. Gradually, I learned responsibility.

Benfica was always the club of my father's heart – and my brother's. But his pride was not diminished by that. To see his son, a native of Madeira, in a Portuguese mainland club, was motive enough to fill him with joy. When I signed for United, he was totally ecstatic. He was with me many, many times, accompanying me, supporting me, encouraging me, right until the moment when he fell ill. We do anything for the people we love. But unfortunately his fate was already determined.

WHEN HE REALIZED EVERYONE AROUND HIM WAS PRAISING ME, HE WOULD NOT UTTER A WORD, COMPLETELY DELIGHTED, EXCITED, AND VERY PROUD

IN THE MATCH
AGAINST RUSSIA
I PLAYED
TO HONOUR
MY FATHER

My father
will always
be in my
heart! . . .

SEPTEMBER 6TH, 2005.

I WAS IN MOSCOW, WITH THE PORTUGUESE NATIONAL TEAM, WHICH WAS PLAYING A 2006 WORLD CUP QUALIFICATION MATCH ON THE NEXT DAY, AGAINST RUSSIA. IT WAS TUESDAY.

I was in my room, watching a movie, when I was summoned by Luiz Felipe Scolari. I went to his room, where Luís Figo, at the time the captain of the Portuguese team, was already waiting. I thought it was odd, but I could never have imagined that the news they had for me was about my father's death. It was a shock for me. I had no feeling. My head felt like a balloon that was suddenly deflated. I could not think about anything. Absolutely nothing.

I COULD NOT THINK ABOUT ANYTHING. ABSOLUTELY NOTHING

"Cristiano, if you want to, go. We will make your flight reservations immediately, and you can go to your family," Luiz Felipe Scolari told me. "No, no, I want to stay here, and I want to play tomorrow," I answered. Those were the first words that sprung to my mind. But they were honest and sincere words. I told him he could rely on me. I told him there were going to be tough moments, but that he could count on me for that game, and that my only wish was to be part of the game. I thought it was the right thing to do. I took that decision for myself, not for other people, or because of other people. I did not wonder if my decision would be better or worse for me, I did not wonder if my presence near my father would help or hurt anyone, or anything. The only thought that crossed my mind was about staying in Moscow and playing against Russia. "I am going to play a game in honour of my father, I will play for him." And so I did.

"I AM GOING TO PLAY A GAME IN HONOUR OF MY FATHER, I WILL PLAY FOR HIM." AND SO I DID

On the day of the match, the mood in the dressing room, and even during the warm-up period, was heavy, it was strange. The behaviour of my team-mates was not normal. They were very quiet, distressed, withdrawn, not knowing what their correct attitude should be. I went to them and explained that they had to act naturally; that they had to be themselves, that it made no sense to alter their behaviour just because of me. I encouraged them to laugh. I felt the need to stimulate them, to lift their spirits. I tried to do exactly the same things that I always did, precisely to put across that message. Anyone who knows Cristiano Ronaldo knows that in the dressing room I am always playing with the ball. Myself and a few other team-mates. For the first time that was not happening so, to relieve the tension and to show them that the team's behaviour should be the same as usual, I started to play with the ball.

It is undeniable that it was hard for me. Very hard. My father filled my thoughts. It is true I tried to score a goal. I try to in every game I play. But this goal would, in fact, be different, it would be special.

Luiz Felipe Scolari, as I have already mentioned, played a decisive role in this moment that was so difficult for me. In fact, even during the training for this game, he gave me permission to go back to London to be near my father, who was then seriously ill. "Never forget that family comes first, and only then comes football," he told me. I refused. At that exact moment my friendship with Scolari began to strengthen. We both cried when he told the story of how his own father died. He was warm, he understood me, he comforted me, he gave me strength.

God wanted my father to go. I felt outraged by his physical disappearance, but that is just the way life is. People die every day, and we know that all of us, one day, will disappear. But when it is a person in our family, everything is much more complicated. Many times, when I am at home, I feel his presence. I cannot explain it, but sometimes I feel that I hear his advice: "Don't do that, don't go that way, that is not the most suitable for you." He is always by my side.

Those were very rough times for me. It is still rough. But we must all follow our own path, we cannot stop. My brothers and sisters and I still feel a void in our lives. Neither I, nor my family, have yet been able to completely overcome this loss. We still love someone who is not physically present, but we must be strong, and keep moving forward. Life is too short to spend with negative, depressive and morbid thoughts. For this reason I do not like to engage in deep conversations about death.

One day I was talking with my mother when, all of a sudden, she made a declaration that caught me completely off guard: "Some day I am going to leave my children, and I will never be able to see them and protect them again." Tears filled my eyes. Why must parents talk about this, after a certain point in their lives? I had to change the subject immediately for, without a doubt, I don't like it, and it makes me feel extremely uncomfortable. Therefore, I believe in the need to make good use of what life has to give us and to enjoy it fully, for it is short. I believe that there may be some kind of life beyond death. We may never meet directly, but that dream will become infinite. Today we are here, in this world, and we should enjoy life to the full. We should welcome everything that comes to us. Without the need of deep philosophical thoughts.

So long father

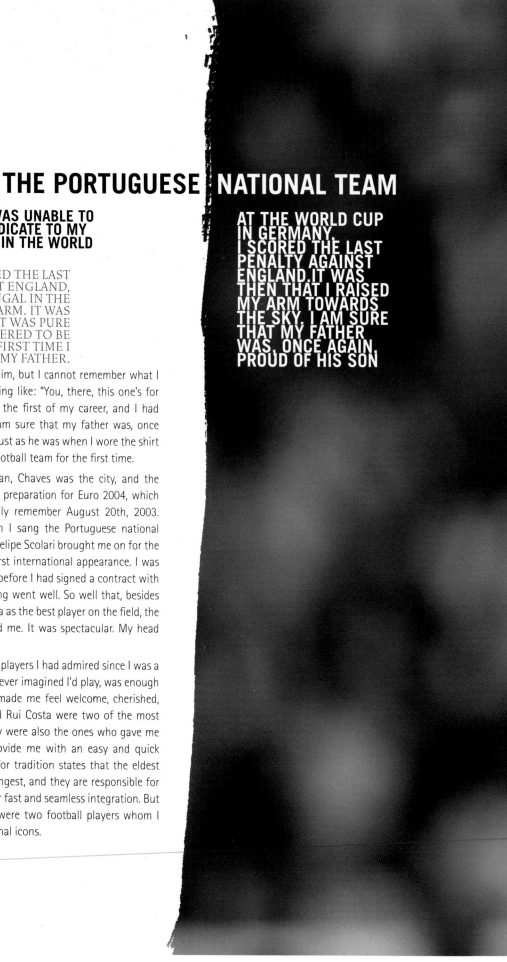

THE PORTUGUESE NATIONAL TEAM

AGAINST RUSSIA, I WAS UNABLE TO SCORE A GOAL TO DEDICATE TO MY FATHER. BUT I DID IT IN THE WORLD CUP IN GERMANY.

I LOOKED AT THE SKY AFTER I SCORED THE LAST PENALTY IN THE MATCH AGAINST ENGLAND, WHICH PUT PORTUGAL IN THE SEMI-FINALS, AND I RAISED MY ARM. IT WAS NOT A PLANNED GESTURE. IT WAS PURE INSTINCT, IN A MOMENT I CONSIDERED TO BE SPECIAL. THIS WAS IN FACT THE FIRST TIME I PUBLICLY HONOURED MY FATHER.

AT THE WORLD CUP IN GERMANY, I SCORED THE LAST PENALTY AGAINST ENGLAND. IT WAS THEN THAT I RAISED MY ARM TOWARDS THE SKY. I AM SURE THAT MY FATHER WAS, ONCE AGAIN, PROUD OF HIS SON

I addressed a few words to him, but I cannot remember what I said. I believe it was something like: "You, there, this one's for you." I was in a World Cup, the first of my career, and I had scored a decisive penalty. I am sure that my father was, once more, very proud of his son. Just as he was when I wore the shirt of the Portuguese national football team for the first time.

The adversary was Kazakhstan, Chaves was the city, and the match was a friendly one, in preparation for Euro 2004, which Portugal would host. I vividly remember August 20th, 2003. Emotion overcame me when I sang the Portuguese national anthem, and also when Luiz Felipe Scolari brought me on for the second half, giving me my first international appearance. I was 18 years old, and a few days before I had signed a contract with Manchester United. Everything went well. So well that, besides being considered by the media as the best player on the field, the national coach congratulated me. It was spectacular. My head was in the clouds.

Being surrounded by football players I had admired since I was a child, and with whom I had never imagined I'd play, was enough to feel privileged. Everyone made me feel welcome, cherished, and supported. Luís Figo and Rui Costa were two of the most experienced players, and they were also the ones who gave me most advice, in order to provide me with an easy and quick adjustment. This is normal, for tradition states that the eldest pass the message to the youngest, and they are responsible for welcoming them and for their fast and seamless integration. But you must understand, they were two football players whom I had always seen as professional icons.

THE ATMOSPHERE ON THE
DAY OF THE FINAL WAS ONE
OF THE MOST SPECTACULAR
I HAVE WITNESSED SINCE I
STARTED TO PLAY FOOTBALL
AND MAYBE EVEN THE MOST
CHILLING

Particularly Luís Figo, for playing in the exact same position as me, and for his playing style. From him I heard these words: "You must feel calm, play normally, do what you know how to do. Imagine you're in your club and not in the national team, and you'll see that everything will be much easier." Good examples must be followed. Today, I try hard to play exactly the same role to the young Portuguese international players that arrive in the national team, without over-emphasising the status I have acquired, due to the success I am having in my career. Our need to belong, in whatever circumstances, is crucial to individual success, but mainly for the team's.

I quickly became "addicted" to the Portuguese national team. A year later I was participating in the first European Championship of my career, with the extra allure of it being hosted by Portugal. I made an impression on the team, and it was also one of the most beautiful moments I've ever lived. For everything: for the union of the Portuguese people, for the training, for the matches, for our companionship and harmony. I remember the first game, in the Dragão Stadium, against Greece, and Luiz Felipe Scolari telling me I was going to play in the second half, then the deep emotion I felt. I committed a foul, which resulted in a penalty and then I scored a goal, my first goal in official matches with the Portuguese national team. I recall the joy of that moment, and the sadness of defeat, at the end of the game. I remember the way we all got together and became a family. The family of the Portuguese national team. There is a particular person responsible for this phenomenon: Luiz Felipe Scolari.

The tears that flowed from my eyes in the final when we lost to Greece, expressed all the disappointment and sadness I felt right then. I looked around me and I saw thousands of broken, disappointed, sad Portuguese people. Witnessing the disappearance

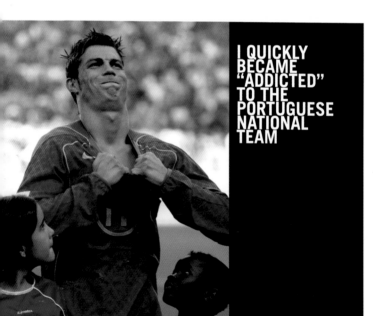

I QUICKLY BECAME "ADDICTED" TO THE PORTUGUESE NATIONAL TEAM

of such a beautiful dream, in such an abrupt and bitter way, moved me. Even more so after we had spent an incredible month, when the Portuguese people had a national spirit that was absolutely sensational and unprecedented.

I never imagined we would lose that cup. But curiously, when Greece knocked out the Czech Republic, we looked at each other with mixed reactions and emotions. "Damn, Greece again? Are we going to end the Championship with the same opponent we started with?" were typical comments. We were confident and we believed that it was possible for us to be European champions, but there was something that just did not feel right.

The atmosphere on the day of the final was one of the most spectacular I have witnessed since I started to play football and maybe even the most chilling. The Lisbon area has a population of about 2.1 million people. I will not say every one of them was out on the streets that day, but I am sure they were more than just thousands, there must have been millions. On foot, by car, motorcycle, bicycle, even by boat (the Tagus river looked so beautiful!). The human cordon that gathered around our bus showed how much hope and adoration they felt for our team. Having lost the final was frustrating for all of us. I cried amid great feelings of sadness. I felt lost. I only wanted to be alone and I stayed alone. I did not even want to watch the video of the game. The next day I left the house only because we were invited to a formal reception by Jorge Sampaio, by then President of the Portuguese

I HAVE BEEN
REPRESENTING
THE PORTUGUESE
NATIONAL
FOOTBALL TEAM
FOR THE LAST
FOUR YEARS,
BUT EACH GAME
I PLAY IS ALWAYS
SPECIAL AND
THE FEELING IS
CONTINUOUSLY
UNIQUE,
REPEATEDLY RICH
IN SATISFACTION

PORTUGAL / IRÃO
17/06/2006

Republic. Gradually, I recovered. After all, we had to understand that our campaign had been good. We lost a great opportunity of winning the European Championship, we deserved it, without a doubt, every critic said so, even our opponents. That afternoon was a terrible frustration for the entire country, but we felt comforted by the manner in which, even after being defeated, fans stood by us. The truth is, we gave a great performance in the European Championship, and the entire football world regarded us with even more respect.

Even today, I still feel the same shivers down my spine as I felt when I sang the Portuguese national anthem for the first time. Hearing it,

BEING PART OF MY COUNTRY'S TEAM IS THE BIGGEST HONOUR . . .

and singing it while wearing the Portuguese national team shirt, is a fantastic experience, and leads me to believe that we can never say "no" to our country. I have been representing the Portuguese national football team for the last four years, but each game I play is always special and the feeling is continuously unique, repeatedly rich in satisfaction. Here, in the Portuguese national team, I feel one hundred per cent Portuguese. Playing for Portugal is absolutely terrific because I love my country.

EVEN TODAY, I STILL FEEL
THE SAME SHIVERS DOWN
MY SPINE AS I FELT WHEN
I SANG THE PORTUGUESE
NATIONAL ANTHEM FOR THE
FIRST TIME

Gooooaaaalllllll . . .

CAPTAIN'S ARMBAND

I AM USUALLY THE LAST MEMBER OF THE TEAM TO ARRIVE ON THE FIELD, EITHER AT UNITED'S GAMES, OR THOSE OF THE PORTUGUESE NATIONAL TEAM.

THIS IS NOT DUE TO ANY KIND OF SUPERSTITION, NOR ON A WHIM, BUT BECAUSE I GOT USED TO IT VERY EARLY ON. HOWEVER, THERE IS NO RULE WITHOUT AN EXCEPTION AND THAT EXCEPTION OCCURRED ON FEBRUARY 6TH, 2007, IN THE EMIRATES STADIUM IN LONDON, ON THE NIGHT PORTUGAL PLAYED A FRIENDLY MATCH AGAINST BRAZIL.

Unlike my normal routine, this time I was the first to come out onto the field, leading my team, the day after my 22nd birthday. There was a major reason for that: for the first time in my career I was handed the captain's armband for Portugal and it was as captain of the team that I walked onto the pitch. I felt somewhat vain, but above all I was very proud. Also because – as I learned later – I was the youngest of all the team's captains in the history of the Portuguese national football team for the last 80 years.

I know that practically every person watching the game, either at the stadium or on television, was surprised. I cannot say that was exactly the case for me. Although I was caught somewhat off guard. Three months earlier, the national coach revealed his intention of promoting me to the position of captain of the Portuguese national team, sometime in the near future – he stated it in a press conference, which took place to announce the shortlist for the match against Kazakhstan, for qualification for Euro 2008.

When I found out about it, my heart started to beat faster. Even though I was aware that his decision to make me captain would not occur immediately, the mere fact that he had suggested my name for such a noble and important purpose was motive enough for me to feel grateful.

That night, in London, the day after my 22nd birthday, I proudly wore the armband on my left arm, almost side by side with the Portuguese escudo embroidered on the shirt and close to my heart. I felt privileged. I was not surprised, considering Luiz Felipe Scolari had already revealed his intentions, but I was able to experience, for the first time, the thrill of wearing that armband. That honour did not bring any extra responsibility, for that is always part of my career, in every training session and in every match I play. The armband did not change anything. Not my character, not the way I play, or the way I am, either on the field or off the field. However, it meant a lot. I enjoyed wearing it very much and it was another step in my development as a football professional.

That was also a special match as it paid homage to a person of whom I was very fond, and whose demise filled every one of us with sadness and longing: Carlos Silva, vice-president of the Portuguese Football Federation. His death left us in deep mourning. For that reason, and for the first time ever, I refused to celebrate my birthday.

My team-mates wanted to sing "Happy Birthday" to me, which always happens when someone's birthday occurs during a training period of the Portuguese national team. "No, I don't want to, because this is not the right moment," I answered. After what had happened, the circumstances were not in fact ideal, so I did not want to have a birthday party. My team-mates respected my wish.

THAT HONOUR DID NOT BRING ANY EXTRA RESPONSIBILITY, FOR THAT IS ALWAYS PART OF MY CAREER . . .

The match went well, even though it was only a friendly in preparation for the competition that followed, which would translate into points. We defeated Brazil and I aimed to do the same as always: to give my best. During the time I was on the field, I did not think too much about what people call "responsibility" due to the fact that I was, on that night, the captain of the team. I always try to behave in the same manner, while wearing the Portuguese national team shirt, or the Manchester United shirt, whether in a match against theoretically lesser opponents, or against teams that are considered to be powerful. I face up to them all in the same way, with the same commitment, the same determination, the same will to win, the same pleasure, the same responsibility.

MUSIC FOR THE EARS AND THE VOICE OF A FUTURE SINGER

MUSIC FOLLOWS ME WHEREVER I GO,
WHETHER IN MY CAR, DURING MY TRIPS
HEADING FOR TRAINING OR THE TOWN
CENTRE, AT HOME WHEN I AM RESTING OR
WHILE I EXERCISE IN THE POOL OR IN THE
GYM. I OWN A WIDE VARIETY OF CD'S TO
BRIGHTEN MY DAYS, NEVER SILENCE. I LIKE A
LITTLE BIT OF EVERYTHING. THE SELECTION
OF MUSICAL GENRES ONLY VARIES DUE TO
THE MOOD OF THE MOMENT, THE COMPANY
OR THE PLACE WHERE I AM.

WITH A FEW "LESSONS" WHO KNOWS IF I CAN MAKE IT?

I also enjoy singing. At home we have a cheerful atmosphere, because between Zé, Nuno, or I, we always know the song lyrics by heart. We even create new words for some tunes. Sometimes it is really funny. It is our way of unwinding, and simultaneously of making time slip easily by.

Obviously, as you will imagine, there are many differences between the player Ronaldo and the singer Ronaldo. But with a few "lessons", who knows if I can make it? At least maybe I can sing well enough to be a part of the chorus for one of my sister Cátia's next CDs. "Ronalda" is her stage name. In all truth, I have already promised her that when she releases her third record, I will sing in one or two songs. No problem.

My sister has been singing since she was very young. She spent her days humming songs everywhere. She performed in a number of concerts with a band called "Galáxia" and we all understood early on that this was the dream of her life. Fortunately for her, it came true. She recorded her second CD, with the title "Esperança" and it is a very good piece of work, which not only reveals her beautiful voice, but also shows her success is not due to the stage name she chose, nor even the fact of being her brother's sister. Gradually Cátia is strengthening her position in the world of music, and her future can only be bright.

As for me, I have no problem in saying that I am her Number One fan. I love her songs. This is why I am always the first person to hear the recordings for every song she does. She makes a point of asking my opinion before the work is released onto the music market. That is what happened once again and what she received was praise.

THE "ANTHEM" FOR THE 2006 WORLD CUP

IN GERMANY DURING THE
WORLD CUP, AFTER EACH
GAME WE WON,
COSTINHA TURNED
INTO A DJ, AND HIS ROOM
INTO A KIND OF DISCO.
I ADOPTED A SONG
DURING THE PERIOD
WE SPENT TOGETHER:
"WORLD, HOLD ON",
BY BOB SINCLAR.

I already liked listening to it before the World Cup, and by the time the World Cup ended, I had made everyone else like it. One of my team-mates recorded a CD with his favourite songs, which included the one that had become "my song". Then, from the back of the bus, only my voice would be heard: "Let's hear number 3, number 3," which was that track's number. And they would humour me by playing it.

The guys got used to that sound. Soon after, I did not even need to ask for the song. As soon as they got on the bus, travelling to training or for a match, they shouted: "Play Cristiano Ronaldo's music! Play Cristiano Ronaldo's music!" And the guys sitting at the front of the bus played the song. But not just once. They played it again and again. Tiago was too much. He would turn to me and say, in a very funny way: "There's Cristiano Róooooonaldo! There's Cristiano Róooooonaldo!" For that was how our affectionate, fantastic emigrants pronounced my name. Bob Sinclar's theme had quickly become my signature tune because everyone understood that the song had a lot of rhythm, and spread joy all around, in a contagious way. In the final phase of the World Cup, even those who at first disliked the tune eventually had it playing on their cell phones . . .

When we returned to Portugal and were enthusiastically received by the Portuguese people, no one forgot the third track of the CD. Travelling on the bus to the National Stadium, as well as when we returned, what did we hear? "World, Hold On", of course – five times! We sang, we clapped our hands, we waved at the crowd, we thanked them for their support, always with the same music playing inside the bus. Watching all that exaltation was catching, for we were not expecting such a grand and warm welcome. It reminded us of the European Championship in 2004. It made us realise that our campaign in the World Cup of 2006 had not been so bad. We ended in fourth place, but we lost to a great team (France). We proved that Portugal is on the right track to make something come true that, until now, has never occurred: winning titles.

DRESSING ROOM FUN

I HAVE ALWAYS BEEN A PLAYFUL PERSON, AND SOMETHING OF A TEASER, BECAUSE I ENJOY LAUGHING. INSIDE MANCHESTER UNITED'S DRESSING ROOM, FOR EXAMPLE, WE HAVE A GREAT TEAM THAT, ALTHOUGH ALWAYS AWARE OF THEIR MANY PROFESSIONAL RESPONSIBILITIES, GET ALONG VERY WELL AND IS ALWAYS READY FOR A GOOD PRANK.

The funnier ones, such as Quintin Fortune (Bolton) or Djemba Djemba (Aston Villa), have already left, but we still have a fantastic atmosphere. Now the laughs are instigated by me, Evra, Rooney or Ferdinand, the gang of "jokers". If anyone comes to the dressing room and asks who is the funniest, I believe most of them will answer that I am. But in fact we all play jokes, whether with someone's earrings, or with another's shoes.

When someone appears with a weird shirt, trousers, or shoes, there is only one thing to do: hang the apparel in a prominent area of the dressing room, for everyone to appreciate the work of art. Or, when we find, in any newspaper or magazine, a photograph of a person who looks like one of us, we cut out the picture, enlarge it and hang it on their locker. We often mimic each other: the grimaces, the manner of speech, the gestures. Evra, for example, is one of those who has fun mimicking me, particularly in game situations. These are harmless jokes, which also contribute to a good healthy working atmosphere.

Evidently, it was not always like this, even though I was always considered a mischievous boy. When I began to play in Andorinha I was very shy. I was afraid to get the ball, because all the other players were taller than me – at the time I played in the little league with boys who were three years older, and that made all the difference. I managed to adjust, and I did not need much time to forge bonds of friendship with the other kids, and give way to my playfulness. It began like this in Andorinha. It went on in Sporting and on the Portuguese national football team, and now that is the way it goes on at Manchester United.

I get along not only with all my team-mates, but also with the coaches and the entire club's staff. I like them, they also like me and I enjoy talking and socializing with them. I also enjoy telling a few jokes. In Manchester I have been with some people for three and a half years – as many years as I have been in the club – and I have obviously taught them (and I still do) many Portuguese words. One of the first words they learnt was "fraquinho". Now we hear them say, in a funny accent: "Good morning, fraquinho". They are not just repeating it, they are not parrots.

They say it because they know what it means, and find it funny. "tudo bem", "bom dia" or "obrigado" are also some of the words they frequently use. Obviously, I have also taught them some slang, but that is common in this environment, and if we think about it, it does no one any harm.

During my first days in the club, roles were reversed: they taught me some English words. We usually hear people say that the language of football is universal, but on the field there are always situations in which we can make use of a few words. As I had some difficulties with the English language, I tried to make myself understood using gestures. At first they would make an odd expression, but with a small effort they could understand me. Today, all that is gone, for I can express myself reasonably well in English, and by now they also know me really well.

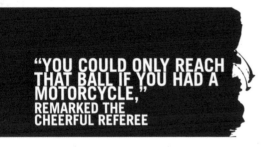

"YOU COULD ONLY REACH THAT BALL IF YOU HAD A MOTORCYCLE," REMARKED THE CHEERFUL REFEREE

This good mood atmosphere often follows us onto the pitch, and even in the heat of competition, it is not unheard of for some jokes to come up during games. I still recall two of those occasions with a smile. A team-mate kicked a long ball in my direction but completely out of my reach, and although I made a good sprint, I could not prevent the ball from going over the line. "You could only reach that ball if you had a motorcycle," remarked the cheerful referee. In another game, an English assistant referee passed by me and said: "Play with a smile on your lips, we like to see you smile." These are absolutely harmless comments, which I know to be also directed at many other players which helps to relieve the tension that exists in high competition. This is another aspect that English football, as well as in the relationships between its various agents, makes a difference.

I also hear some comments from opponent players that bring a smile to my face. It happened recently during the last Manchester United–Roma match, when we were already winning 6–0: "Don't do any more dribbles, you are already winning by six", said one of them, almost begging. Obviously I will not reveal his name, these are nothing but mere comments, brought about by the occurrences of the game. Others, like some right-wingers who play in England, ask me to go and play on the opposite side; and others do not show any sense of humour when they make threats to my physical integrity. I know they are merely trying to scare me, nothing more. But these comments are worthless, for I keep on playing exactly in the same way. I just whistle and play with the team.

Some people do not like training camps on the days before games. I consider them important, for they provide greater concentration and tranquillity for what really matters: a good performance on the day of the match. This does not mean that it could not happen if we stayed at home, but I find that the concentration is in fact different. As long as they are not excessive, I believe training camps are important for the relaxing period that a foot-ball professional needs before a game. I like training camps, and I also enjoy the team spirit that exists during those periods. At Manchester United, for example, the game console is one of the objects we often use to play football matches, or action games, and everyone has a good time. I do it too, of course. "Get down, go forward, nowslide to the right, no, no, to the left," they tell each other. I find that funny, and the interaction strengthens the team spirit.

In the Portuguese national football team the atmosphere is also fantastic, but we occupy our spare time in a different way. We have fun playing cards, and get enthusiastic about it. We play "copas", and my group is almost always the same. During the World Cup, for example, with me were Deco, Maniche, Postiga, Figo and Paulo Santos, one of the funniest in the group. And I can say we put up a good fight. It is a different atmosphere indeed. Not better, not worse: it is just different. It is more intimate, because we all speak the same language, and also because we have many things in common. I feel like I am at home.

I LIKE TRAINING CAMPS, AND I ALSO ENJOY THE TEAM SPIRIT THAT EXISTS DURING THOSE PERIODS

MADEIRA ISLAND AND MY FRIEND ALBERTO JOÃO JARDIM

MADEIRA IS THE MOST BEAUTIFUL ISLAND IN THE WORLD, AND IT IS CONSIDERED
THE "PEARL OF THE ATLANTIC". I DO NOT SAY THIS BECAUSE I WAS BORN THERE,
SPENT PART OF MY CHILDHOOD THERE, OR BECAUSE I FEEL AT HOME THERE. I SAY
IT BECAUSE IT IS INDEED A SPECIAL AND MAGICAL PLACE.

BEING DISTINGUISHED BY THE GOVERNMENT OF MY DISTRICT WAS A MOMENT OF GREAT PRIDE AND EMOTION

Those who know the island understand what I mean and those who visit wish to return as soon as possible. There is a reason why Madeira is a first choice tourist destination.

I fondly remember Quinta do Falcão and Bairro de Santo António, those were the places I grew up in, where I made my first friendships, and also where I first started to kick a ball. And I remember Funchal, where I accompanied my mother when she went shopping for the home. Madeira, with its different attractions, is undoubtedly one of the most seductive islands in the world.

When I was in Sporting, I yearned for the day I would return to Madeira, to play for the first time in my homeland, wearing the shirt of my new club. That day came when I was still playing in the junior team, I was then 15 or 16 years old. We had reached the second phase of the championship and the draw determined that, from the four teams we had to play against, Marítimo was one of them. More than that, the match was scheduled to be held on Campo de Santo António, that is, almost beside my block and the house I was born in. As soon as I knew the result of the draw, the first thing I did was call home. "Mother, guess who is playing against Sporting?", I asked in one breath. "Tell me, my son," my mother answered. "It's Marítimo, and the match is going to be there, in Campo de Santo António!" I told her, very happily. "You don't say!" my mother yelled, also filled with joy.

It was delirious. My family and my friends did not lose any time. They immediately started to arrange preparations for a big party, with the purpose of giving me a glorious reception when I returned to Madeira. I was also quite excited. But all this joy and excitement were gone in a second. When, on the next Friday, the call-up was posted and I could not find my name on it, I was taken over by a flood of emotions. First I thought I had missed it, and I read all the names again, one by one. Nothing. I rubbed my eyes and I read again. Nothing. I could not believe it. So Sporting was going to Madeira, and precisely on the one game that would make me return, I had not been called-up? I began to cry compulsively, a river of tears. They were all expecting me, relatives and friends, to support Sporting and I . . . would remain alone in Lisbon. I would not play, I would not experience the sensation of my first return home, not be able to bring that joy to my family and my friends. My first reaction was to run to the telephone. "Mum, I wasn't called-up, I want to leave this place," I said among all the sobbing. My mother also began to cry, but once again she gave me plenty of advice. "You have to understand, Ronaldo", she told me. "If you were here I would punish you, too", she added. The reason was, my passion for football was damaging my school progress. More precisely, I rarely arrived at classes on time. The people responsible for Sporting knew that I wanted to be on that specific game more than anything in the world, and they decided to punish me severely: they took from me what I wanted most. It was very hard to bear. But I admit it was the best thing they could have done. From there on, I only got better.

When I look back, I cannot help but feel astonished by the growth that Madeira has undergone, at all levels. During the last ten years, it has developed in an amazing manner. Even I, as young as I still am, notice this evolution each time I return to the island. I can imagine what the people from my parent's generation might say. This evolutionary phenomenon of the whole region has a face and a name: Alberto João Jardim.

It is undeniable that he is a special person, if only for his peculiar personality. I do not fancy discussing politics, nor do I admit to being associated with party A, B, or C. That is not the question. What truly matters is the quality of his work, and that is unquestionable and has been for years. Furthermore, he is an amazing person, to whom the word monotony does not exist. I met him when I was 16 years old, and what caught my attention at that moment was his deep knowledge of football.

He congratulated me when I went to Sporting, and afterwards he invited me to visit his official residence, to get to know me and to tell me that he is very proud of me. I deeply admire this man who guides the destiny of Madeira. One may agree with him, one may not agree with him – no one knows the truth – but one cannot deny that straightforwardness is one of his virtues for, as it is usually said, he is not tongue-tied. Along with all these features, he is a very funny person. I can say that every moment spent with him is unique. From his own hands I received the Autonomic Region Valour Award, the highest individual honour ever granted to a native of Madeira. I felt privileged. Receiving such a prestigious award, and being distinguished by the Government of my district, was a moment of great pride and emotion.

JORGE SAMPAIO, THE MAN WHO LEFT A BIGGER IMPRESSION

ALBERTO JOÃO JARDIM WAS ONE OF THE PERSONALITIES I HAD THE PLEASURE OF BEING INTRODUCED TO. JORGE SAMPAIO, WHO WAS PRESIDENT OF THE PORTUGUESE REPUBLIC BETWEEN 1996 AND 2006, WAS ANOTHER.

As soon as the Portuguese national football team was knocked out of the European Championship of 2004, the presidency of the Portuguese Republic paid homage to all the members of the committee of the national football team, competition finalists. During the dinner to which we were invited, I was sitting on a different table, when he took the initiative of calling me over to sit near him. I admit I did not expect him to do that, but in this way I got to know him better. After having had a long conversation, I knew that not only had I been with a naturally intelligent person – hardly news to me – but also somebody who had a higher than average take on sports culture – and this indeed surprised me. When I say interest in sports culture I do not mean exclusively football. I include practically all sports, and he knew a little about all of them. I was very pleased to meet him, and I place Jorge Sampaio in the gallery of personalities who impressed me the most.

Meeting Alberto João Jardim and Jorge Sampaio meant the possibility of establishing personal contact with two personalities of undeniable standing, whom I admire very much. Who besides them would I like to meet? I have been asked that question a few times, and my reply may seem a little odd, but is absolutely true: I would like to meet the person who invented the aeroplane. Obviously I know it is not possible for that wish to come true. On the one hand, because he is no longer among the living, and on the other hand, I have read that doubts exist about who accomplished it. Some say it was the Brazilian Santos Dumont, and others insist that it was the Wright brothers, from the U.S.A. Whoever it was, I would love to have met the man and talked to him about how he felt for having been the first to imitate birds.

When I was a child, I often raised my eyes towards the sky as soon as I heard the sound of the motors of these beautiful monsters of the air, which nowadays, thanks to the constant progress of engineering, naturally cannot be compared to those which made those first flights.

The moment I experienced the sensations of my first aeroplane trip was exciting. I was 12 then. In the company of my mother, the journey between Funchal and Lisbon aroused in me, above all, enormous curiosity – the wish to know, to see or to learn exists even today. I began the trip with great enthusiasm, eager to learn how everything worked. With my small head glued to the windowpane when the aeroplane started to gain altitude, I had eyes only for the outside, curious to see my beautiful island from above, looking for my house, memorising every detail. However, my enthusiasm vanished as the plane gained more and more altitude. I started to cry, longing for my family. All curiosity was gone. My eyes could only see the image of my brothers, who had said goodbye to me at the airport a short while before. They were all wearing sunglasses, with very dark lenses, but not even that prevented tears from escaping their eyes. The aeroplane kept gaining height and all I could recall was that moment. I wept even more and to make matters worse, I started to feel terrible pain in my ears. I got so sick that I even threw up. I did not enjoy my first experience among the clouds. However, it would be the only time it happened, and today I take pleasure in travelling by aeroplane.

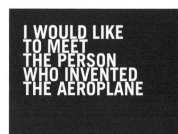
I WOULD LIKE TO MEET THE PERSON WHO INVENTED THE AEROPLANE

In the desert,
Dubai

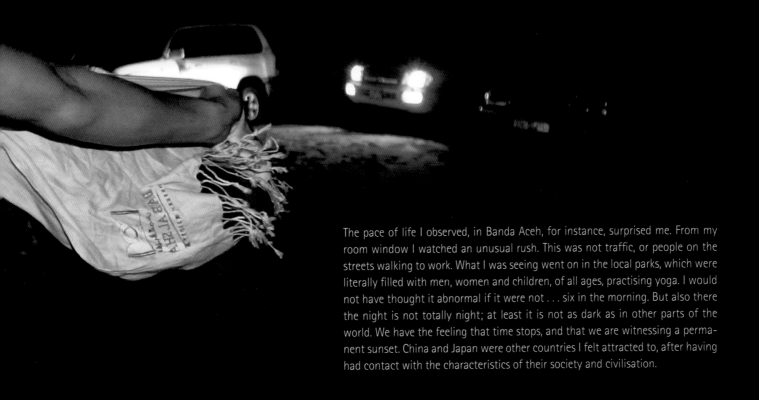

VACATIONS

MANY OF THE TRIPS I HAVE MADE HAVE BEEN LONG-DISTANCE, WHICH CAN MOSTLY BE EXPLAINED BY THE VARIOUS PUBLICITY CONTRACTS I SIGN.

THEY WERE ALL UNFORGETTABLE MOMENTS, NOT ONLY FOR THE PLEASURE I HAVE ADMITTEDLY FELT WHILE WORKING ON THOSE CAMPAIGNS, BUT ALSO BECAUSE THEY ALLOW ME TO GET TO KNOW OTHER CULTURES. I WAS DELIGHTED WITH ASIA, ESPECIALLY BALI, INDONESIA, WHERE I HAD THE OPPORTUNITY TO ENJOY A FEW DAYS IN ABSOLUTE REST AND TRANQUILLITY.

The pace of life I observed, in Banda Aceh, for instance, surprised me. From my room window I watched an unusual rush. This was not traffic, or people on the streets walking to work. What I was seeing went on in the local parks, which were literally filled with men, women and children, of all ages, practising yoga. I would not have thought it abnormal if it were not . . . six in the morning. But also there the night is not totally night; at least it is not as dark as in other parts of the world. We have the feeling that time stops, and that we are witnessing a permanent sunset. China and Japan were other countries I felt attracted to, after having had contact with the characteristics of their society and civilisation.

I love to travel, getting to know new places, I like to watch and discover the customs of other people: how they are, what they do, how they live. I always end up drawing important elements from these experiences with other races. Invariably, I am left with the feeling that they have contributed a little more towards my intellectual enrichment. This not only occurs when I travel due to reasons linked to my professional activities, but also when the pretext is simply to enjoy a few days' vacation.

My wishes are not very different from those common to all the people who crave a few quiet hours after a year of intense working stress. At the moment I choose the destination, however, I have a major concern: finding a peaceful place and a hotel room with a SPA that can offer the necessary conditions to a person who needs to coordinate leisure with some exercise; indispensable to an athlete, even during his vacations.

I LOVE TO TRAVEL, GETTING TO KNOW NEW PLACES, I LIKE TO WATCH AND DISCOVER THE CUSTOMS OF OTHER PEOPLE

I ALWAYS END UP DRAWING IMPORTANT ELEMENTS FROM THESE EXPERIENCES WITH OTHER RACES. INVARIABLY, I AM LEFT WITH THE FEELING THAT THEY HAVE CONTRIBUTED A LITTLE MORE TOWARDS MY INTELLECTUAL ENRICHMENT

EVERY VACATION I TAKE IS SPECIAL, FOR I ENJOY IT TO THE MAXIMUM, AND IT IS ALWAYS DIFFERENT, THEREFORE IT IS IMPOSSIBLE FOR ME TO CHOOSE ONE OVER THE OTHER. THE PERIOD I SPENT IN PALMA DE MALLORCA, FORMENTERA, AND IBIZA (SPAIN) WAS MAYBE ONE OF THE MERRIER I HAVE HAD UP TO NOW. WE HAD SUN, SEA, AND WE SAILED. IT WAS REALLY GREAT. WHETHER IT WAS THE BEST OR NOT, I CANNOT SAY IN ALL HONESTY

I love the sun, therefore, for me, vacation is synonymous with beach. I love to feel the sand on my hands, my feet, and even on my body. I like to lay on the towel, totally relaxed and not thinking about anything at all. I like to dive in the sea and I love to swim. I enjoy watching the sunset, and contemplating the sea, for that is how I feel truly relaxed, without any kind of pressure. Looking at the sea reminds me of Madeira, my home, the activity of boats in Funchal harbour. The fun and games that I still play with my friends during vacations also take me back to my childhood. I am usually accompanied by the same friends: Zé, Nuno, sometimes my brother and cousins, and some people from Gestifute. I do not have many friends, but I pride myself on them being firm friends. When we are all together, we look like children without a care in the world, having fun and happy doing something as simple as playing in the water.

I LOVE THE SUN,
THEREFORE, FOR
ME, VACATION IS
SYNONYMOUS
WITH BEACH

I LIKE TO DIVE IN THE SEA AND I LOVE TO SWIM

Often the simplest things in life are also the most beautiful. We need to value them.

Every vacation I take is special, for I enjoy it to the maximum, and it is always different, there-fore it is impossible for me to choose one over the other. The period I spent in Palma de Mallorca, Formentera, and Ibiza (Spain) was maybe one of the merrier I have had up to now. We had sun, sea, and we sailed. It was really great. Whether it was the best or not, I cannot say in all honesty.

THE AUSTRALIAN
CONTINENT
HAS A SPECIAL
MEANING FOR ME.
IT HAS BEEN THE
HOME OF MY
GRANDFATHER
FOR MANY
YEARS NOW,
BUT I NEVER
HAD A CHANCE
TO VISIT

With my family and my friends, every moment of rest has been fantastic, especially in Madeira, which is obviously one of my frequent destinations. Last summer, for instance, I spent most of my holidays there, and I always reserve at least five or six days, every year, to be there. That is my home.

Not very long ago, I visited Dubai, considered by many to be the New York of the desert, and it may probably be true. I had already been there three years before, in a break with Manchester United, but this time I had the opportunity of spending five days of total relaxation, in the company of my long-time friends. I loved it. Dubai's architectural richness, which I could appreciate better this time, impressed me. The population's quality of living, cultural diversity and the beauty of this Islamic country makes me want to repeat the experience. The climate is magnificent – the sunshine and the high temperatures are constant throughout the year – and the coast presents a dazzling sea of crystal clear waters. I was also in the desert, where, for the first time, I rode a camel. It was amusing, even though I did not get too enthusiastic about it, mainly for being somewhat uncomfortable. But the mere fact of being in the middle of a vast expanse of sand, with nothing around but a hotel, was a different vision from anything I had yet seen. Listening to the silence and contemplating millions of stars in the black sky was an image of rare beauty, not comparable to

WITH MY FAMILY AND MY FRIENDS EVERY MOMENT OF REST HAS BEEN FANTASTIC

the restlessness of large urban centres we are all used to. Dubai was truly one of the most complete places I have had the opportunity of knowing.

In the future, I hope to visit Miami, New York and Australia. Australia has a special meaning for me. That is where my maternal grandfather has been living for many years, and I have never had the opportunity to visit him. That grandfather, as I recall, had serious doubts about my parents deciding to let me go to Sporting. "The boy, is he going alone to the Portuguese mainland? That can't be!" he complained, fearful of what could happen to me. I know that today he bursts with pride for his grandson.

LIFE ISN'T
JUST
FOOTBALL

THE MERE
FACT OF BEING
IN THE MIDDLE
OF A VAST
EXPANSE OF
SAND, WITH
NOTHING
AROUND BUT
A HOTEL, WAS
A DIFFERENT
VISION FROM
ANYTHING I
HAD YET SEEN

I was thrilled by the desert

HUMILITY IS ONE OF THE VALUES I MOST CHERISH, AS WELL AS EDUCATION AND INSTRUCTION. ON THE DAY I HAVE A CHILD, THOSE ARE THE MAIN PRINCIPLES I WILL PASS ON TO HIM, FOR I CONSIDER THAT, FROM THERE ON, EVERYTHING ELSE WILL COME NATURALLY.

THE IDEA OF HAVING A CHILD STIRS TWO DISTINCT FEELINGS IN ME: IT FRIGHTENS ME, FOR THE RESPONSIBILITY IT REPRESENTS, BUT ON THE OTHER HAND IT IS EXCITING, AND THIS MAY EVEN SEEM CONTRADICTORY. BUT IT IS NOT. I OBVIOUSLY WANT TO BECOME A FATHER. BUT NOT NOW, IS IT TOO SOON FOR ME FOR I AM STILL VERY YOUNG. I ALSO DO NOT INTEND TO GET MARRIED NOW, NOR IN THE NEAR FUTURE. RIGHT NOW I AM OF THE RIGHT AGE TO DATE, AND I CAN DO IT BECAUSE I AM NOT PLEDGED TO ANYONE. THE THIRTIES SEEM TO ME LIKE A PROPER AGE TO TAKE ON A COMMITMENT AS SERIOUS AS MARRIAGE.

GETTING MARRIED AND HAVING A CHILD

This does not mean that I cannot take that step at an earlier age – we never know what may happen tomorrow – but in all truth it does not figure in my immediate plans. However, I would like to have a child some time before getting married and if it is a boy, then he should have the same "football" genes as me, so that he can follow in my footsteps. If he looked like me, it would be even better. I will not say I would like to have a clone, but hope that our similarities would be easy to notice, at all levels. It would be pleasant to have offspring with the same characteristics as his father, one who may become a football player and build a great career. It would be spectacular. For now, I dream about that day, but for the moment I do not want to go beyond the limit of the dream. But one day, a day still far way, who knows?

During my sleep I usually dream a lot, and generally remember everything when I wake up. Curiously, one of the last dreams I have had almost turned into a nightmare: I dreamed I was getting married. I do not know to whom, for I cannot recall her face. I just remember that my "bride" was a beautiful woman, whom I loved very much. Just that. I remember my mother's joy, and the happiness of the people who surrounded me. I also recall that I was not a boy, but already a man. That was when I woke up. I felt great relief, but also deep pain, for I had just slammed my head against the wardrobe that is near my bed. Right then I realised that it was all a dream. What a relief!

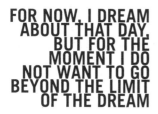

FOR NOW, I DREAM ABOUT THAT DAY, BUT FOR THE MOMENT I DO NOT WANT TO GO BEYOND THE LIMIT OF THE DREAM

IT IS 7:30 AM, THE ALARM CLOCK HAS JUST RUNG. I GET UP, I GET DRESSED, I GO DOWN TO THE KITCHEN. THIS TIME I HAVE YOGHURT, I PREPARE A CHEESE AND HAM GRILLED SANDWICH AND TOAST, AND I LEAVE THE HOUSE. I TAKE ABOUT 25 MINUTES TO REACH MANCHESTER UNITED'S TRAINING CENTRE.

TRAINING IS SCHEDULED FOR 10 AM, BUT AS I HAVE ALREADY EXPLAINED, I PREFER TO ARRIVE VERY EARLY: I LIKE TO GET READY WITHOUT HAVING TO RUSH, I LIKE TO PLAY WITH THE BALL, TO EXERCISE AT THE CLUB'S GYM, AND TO WORK WITH THE TEAM.

Sometimes I have breakfast there. Training lasts for two hours, so I return home around 1 pm. I eat lunch, and generally stay at home. I only go out again when it is training camp day: usually assembly is scheduled for 6 pm at Old Trafford, where we all meet before going to the hotel, or before travelling when games are not at home.

This time I was responsible for lunch. I mean, I helped Zé and Nuno. I made the salad, which is a part of every meal, and I helped with the last finishing touches of the meal, in this case a delicious roast chicken. For sheer pleasure, not as an obligation, once in a while I go to the kitchen and cook a dish, but only occasionally, on my free days. Otherwise we would only have lunch in the middle of the afternoon, for I never return from training before 1 pm. Nuno also

DAILY ROUTINE:
HOME—TRAINING—HOME

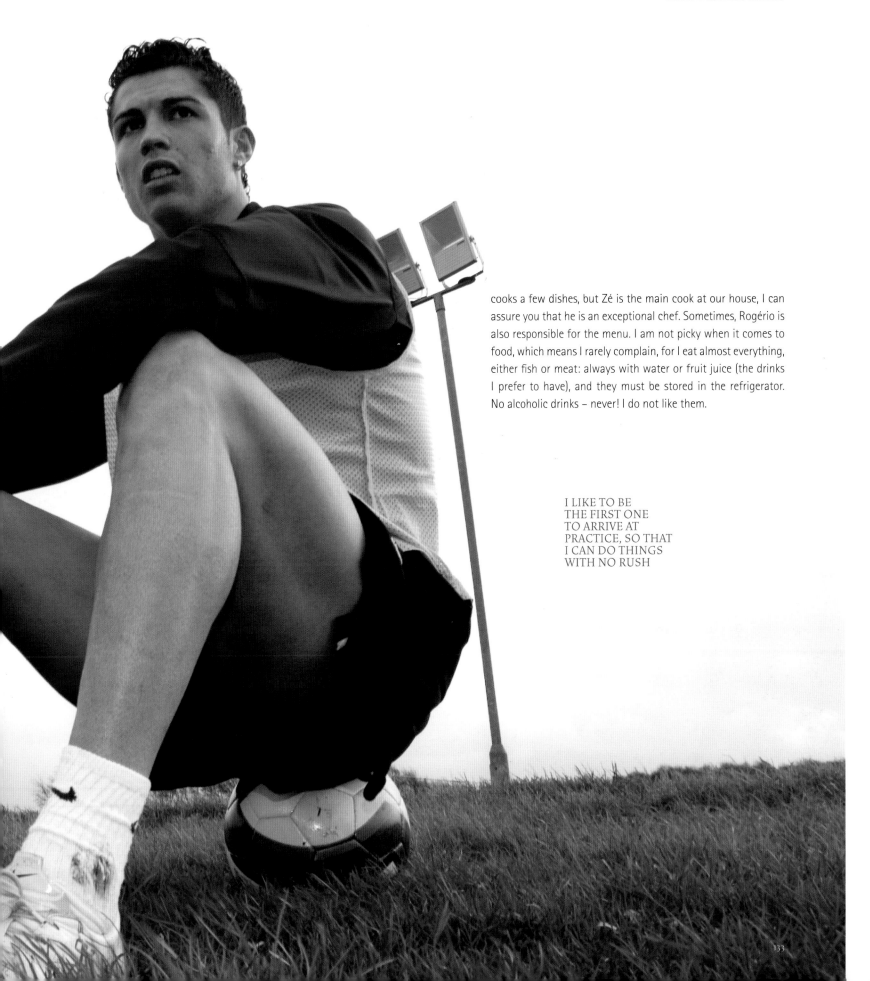

cooks a few dishes, but Zé is the main cook at our house, I can assure you that he is an exceptional chef. Sometimes, Rogério is also responsible for the menu. I am not picky when it comes to food, which means I rarely complain, for I eat almost everything, either fish or meat: always with water or fruit juice (the drinks I prefer to have), and they must be stored in the refrigerator. No alcoholic drinks – never! I do not like them.

I LIKE TO BE
THE FIRST ONE
TO ARRIVE AT
PRACTICE, SO THAT
I CAN DO THINGS
WITH NO RUSH

DURING THE FIRST TWO YEARS WITH
MANCHESTER UNITED, MY FAMILY MADE
A POINT OF BEING A CONSTANT PHYSICAL
PRESENCE IN MY LIFE, SPECIFICALLY
MY MOTHER, MY SISTER CÁTIA AND MY
BROTHER-IN-LAW ZÉ

Day after day, this is my routine, necessarily different from what I did in Portugal. During the first two years with Manchester United, my family made a point of being a constant physical presence in my life, specifically my mother, my sister Cátia and my brother-in-law Zé. In them I found all the support I needed and thanks to them I never knew the meaning of the word loneliness. It could not have happened any other way: I was an 18-year-old boy, newly arrived in a foreign country, and none of them would consider the possibility of leaving me unprotected. Their presence helped to shorten the distance, and reduced the longing I felt for home, which often made me feel bad during the first years I lived in Lisbon. The family was once again paramount, especially for their invaluable help in solving a few logistic matters, for which I absolutely needed to master the English language.

When I arrived in England, I talked as little as possible, so I felt the need to have some English lessons, to make my adjustment to this new challenge a little bit easier. The teacher came to my house almost every day, but after four or five months I gave up the classes. I felt I already knew the basics, and I began to feel tired, and also impatient. However I must say, in my defence, that a number of circumstances contributed to that: in the dressing room of Manchester United there were two players who spoke Spanish, therefore I talked to them; on games days, the translator was the bridge between me and the coach, telling me what I should do on the field; during interviews, the presence of the translator was also assured; when it was necessary to take care of more specific matters, I counted on the valuable help of Zé and Cátia, who could speak English quite well. This meant that I never felt any real need to master the language. What I knew was enough to cover my daily needs, that is, I could make myself understood in simple matters. As I had everything "made" for me, I chose the easy way. I believe the scenario would have been very different had I been alone in Manchester. Then I would have needed to express myself for everything, which would have forced me to learn English in a more intensive way.

I returned to the English lessons again, five or six months before the beginning of the World Cup in 2006, with the purpose of perfecting the language. I had recognised the importance of mastering English, so I made an effort during that year and I succeeded. Now I understand everything I am told, and I can make myself clearly understood, even when talking with the media. I no longer need the crutch of a translator. Not only am I totally aware that now I am on the right track, but I also believe, before long, I will be able to speak perfect English. My will to learn is not limited to the language of Shakespeare. I also intend to learn French and Italian, two other languages that fascinate me.

Not exactly a "chef". Usually I just help Zé and Nuno

FOR SHEER PLEASURE, NOT AS AN OBLIGATION, ONCE IN A WHILE I GO TO THE KITCHEN AND COOK A DISH, BUT ONLY OCCASIONALLY

I NOW LIVE IN A QUIET PLACE, UNLIKE DURING THE FIRST TWO YEARS

At the moment, my house is a bachelor pad. I live with Nuno and Zé who, besides being relatives, are two friends whom I love. I like all my cousins, but Nuno is a special cousin. I have the same affinity with my brother-in-law Zé, one of the people I trust the most. They are the ones who truly know Cristiano Ronaldo, the only people who know what I do or don't do, only they know my most intimate side. For that reason we three live together in Manchester. My mother often visits me and, if need be, she will spend a whole month with me, for she is always present in my life.

We are a family, and as such we do practically everything together. We lead a quiet life, which is the way we like it. During the first two years, when my mother was permanently with me, we sometimes lunched in a restaurant, and in the afternoon we would take long walks, to get to know the city. I cannot help but smile when I recall the many pavements I mounted when I tried the new experience of driving on the left, something I was not used to. However, three or four months later, the clumsiness vanished, and I became adjusted to the new rules, to the great relief of my passengers . . .

I now live in a quiet place, unlike during the first two years. I was closer to the centre of Manchester then, but I was beginning to lose my privacy. I moved, not on a whim, but due to the need to live in a more pleasant, secluded and protected place. I also needed a space that could provide me with good leisure facilities, since I spend most of the day at home. I enjoy having this style of comfort.

I believe that this depiction of a quiet, stay-at-home Cristiano Ronaldo goes against the image that most people have of me. It is, however, the plain truth. I do not walk around, I am not a "bon-vivant", I do not often go out . The people who really know me will tell you that I am a very quiet person who enjoys the simple things of life: I enjoy staying at home, watching television, listening to music, and I like to rest. Furthermore, resting is a key-word in my daily life, for I consider it fundamental to my line of work. As everyone knows, the career of a football professional is quite short. If he is able to take care of himself properly, during the years he takes part in top competition not only will he add immensely to his competitive edge, but he might even be able to extend his active career. This is precisely my motto for life.

Being home means relaxing, with family and friends

Obviously, I sometimes go into the centre of Manchester, I also have lunch or dinner in restaurants. But usually I prefer to stay home, surrounded by friends, surrounded by family. Quietly, without any pressure.

It is cold, and it rains continuously. The outer gate broke due to the intensity of the wind. I arrive home earlier, for the storm that hit England today did not allow us to train on the pitch, and even the cover of the pavilion at the training centre could not cope with the bad weather. There are fallen trees almost everywhere, some of which have damaged the electricity cables. Even so, after fulfilling a long-standing appointment, an interview for the French magazine *L'Equipe*, I return home, and it is completely in darkness, with no electricity. The candles we have at home are insufficient, so we are back on the road, now heading toward the nearest supermarket.

USUALLY I PREFER TO STAY HOME, SURROUNDED BY FRIENDS, SURROUNDED BY FAMILY. QUIETLY, WITHOUT ANY PRESSURE

It is not unusual for me to accompany Zé and Nuno when they go shopping for the home. I am not saying it is regular practice, but I have no problem in doing it occasionally. This time we need candles. Our trip is in vain, for everyone in the neighbourhood thought exactly the same, so candles had sold out. After signing a few autographs, we head towards another supermarket. This time we come out with a huge load of candles. Back home, we spread them throughout all the rooms, even on the steps of the stairs that lead to the first floor. The result was wonderful, but it did not surprise me, for occasionally I enjoy the tranquillity and peace of mind that a candle-lit atmosphere can bring.

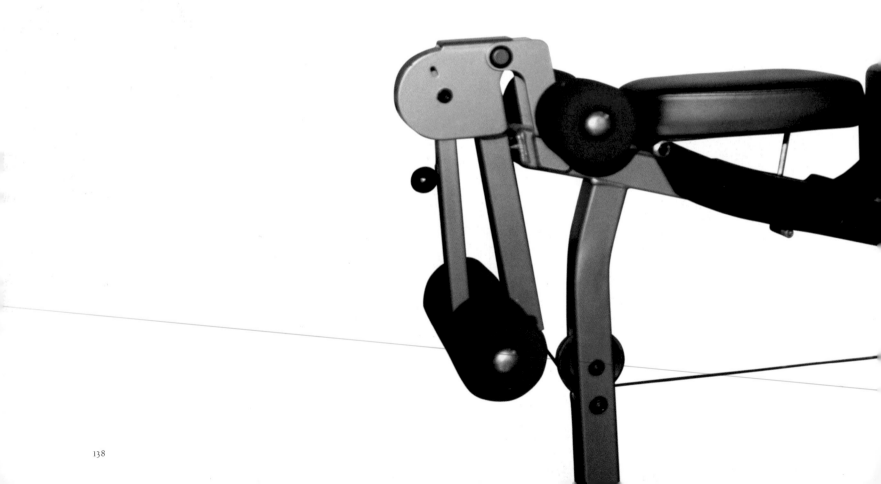

PING-PONG

WHAT TO DO NOW? PRACTICALLY THE SAME AS ALWAYS. I GET THE PING-PONG TABLE READY; WHILE ZÉ BEGINS PREPARATIONS FOR DINNER, I PLAY A GAME WITH NUNO.

After football, ping-pong (and athletics) is my favourite sport. I am delighted to watch professional matches, and I love to play. This fascination for ping-pong began very early in my life, and it can be explained by the fact that it is a very popular sport in Madeira, where there are several clubs, extremely competitive on a national level, such as São Roque, Estreito or Câmara de Lobos. I started to practise it as a small boy, both in my neighbourhood and at school. I never stopped playing, even when I moved to the Sporting Academy.

To my satisfaction, there were plenty of ping-pong tables in the area that is common to all athletes at the training centre. Even when I played in the starters' team, I often went down to the floor below and had some fun with my colleagues. Until, one day, the coach of the Sporting ping-pong team saw me play and came up to me. "I have seen you play, and I think you may become a good ping-pong player. Do you want to practice it?" he asked me. "No, no thanks," I answered in one breath. "What I want is to be a football player. Ping-pong is just a diversion, a hobby, not a sport to build a career, or to become a professional," I explained. I could not convince him at that time. He was so enthusiastic about me that he tried to persuade me again and again. However, I always refused, and he eventually gave up. Football was my passion. I do not know if ping-pong has lost a good player or not. But I do know that even today I enjoy playing it. For sheer fun. I play with my right hand, then with my left hand, and without meaning to boast, I think I do quite well. Nuno does not stand a chance. And even those who believe they have a certain knack for it have to believe the evidence.

I DO NOT KNOW IF PING-PONG HAS LOST A GOOD PLAYER OR NOT. BUT I DO KNOW THAT EVEN TODAY I ENJOY PLAYING IT

TENNIS

THE NIGHT IS FALLING, WE STILL HAVE NO ELECTRICITY, THE WIND HAS CALMED DOWN, BUT IT IS TOO COLD FOR ME TO RISK A TENNIS MATCH.

In fact, only when days begin to warm up a little do I dare to step out of the house and challenge my friends to a tennis match. I cannot say I play as well as I play ping-pong but I do enjoy playing very much. I also like watching it, particularly the Grand Slam tournaments. I appreciate the most competitive players, such as Roger Federer or Rafael Nadal. I like Andre Agassi very much, but Andy Roddick may well be my favourite tennis player.

From my garden, right beside the tennis court, I can see squirrels, peacocks, and even some cows grazing. These are my quiet neighbours, who have already become used to this healthy and peaceful cohabitation, with no mutual interference. But as it is very cold, I look across at them through the window.

I APPRECIATE THE MOST COMPETITIVE PLAYERS, SUCH AS ROGER FEDERER OR RAFAEL NADAL

141

FOR THE FIRST TIME IN A LONG TIME, THERE IS NO MUSIC PLAYING IN THE HOUSE, BECAUSE WE STILL HAVE NO ELECTRICITY.

WE CANNOT PLAY PING-PONG, FOR THE NIGHT IS FALLING AND THE CANDLELIGHT, ALTHOUGH BEAUTIFUL, DOES NOT ALLOW US TO SEE THE LITTLE BALL CLEARLY ENOUGH. SO I HEAD TOWARDS THE SWIMMING POOL; I USE IT EVERY DAY, AT ALL HOURS OF THE DAY. I ENJOY SWIMMING VERY MUCH. I REALLY DO ENJOY IT.

SWIMMING

When I was a boy, the beach was one of the places I frequently went to. I fondly recall the Lido beach, and Formosa beach, both near Funchal. Formosa is composed of several small islands and after a while, I acquired the daily habit of swimming from the beach to one of those islands. Morning and afternoon, I swam from the beach to the rock, and from the rock to the beach, several times, without getting tired. Feeling happy, because I always enjoyed swimming.

Today, swimming is also a habit. I have some good swims in the pool at my house, which could even be considered a supplement to the daily workout I do at Manchester United. Besides providing an excellent relaxation, swimming is probably the most complete training activity there is, since it works the entire body in the same manner, that is to say, it exercises every muscle. In England football matches follow each other relentlessly, so swimming is the ideal opportunity to relax, and simultaneously to develop physical fitness.

On the upper floor of the pool area I have some exercise equipment, but I seldom use it. A long time ago, I escaped to the gym, in the Sporting Academy, and jumped on the body-building machines. At the time I was 14 or 15 years old, I was very skinny and I thought that if I exercised on that equipment, it would be easier for me to build muscle. Three times a week, after nightfall and without anyone knowing, a couple of friends and I jumped over the fence, climbed on to the roof and went down to the gymnasium. We practised weight-lifting and we ran on the treadmill, usually for approximately 40 minutes. The problem was, someone noticed us, and reported us to the person responsible for the gym. The result was that the gym was locked up and we were forbidden from returning there.

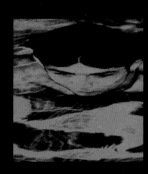

This taste for physical fitness, I can assure you, cannot be interpreted as any kind of body worship. That attitude was due only to my wish to become stronger, for I was really thin. Today that does not happen. I know that our image is highly valued nowadays, not only with regard to football but also in areas such as marketing or advertising. It is also evident that this new generation cares more about their appearance, unlike in the past. I wore braces for a year to straighten my teeth, and I did not like the experience but I got used to them because I needed to, and because, above all, I enjoy feeling good about myself.

DO NOT MISTAKE THE
PLEASURE OF PHYSICAL
EXERCISE FOR AN
OBSESSION WITH THE
BODY

When he saw my legs and my feet, the obstetrician who delivered me apparently made a comment that was, to say the least, curious: "Dona Dolores, your son has the feet of a football player. This little boy is going to bring you a lot of joy." My mother was impressed, for she had always had a passion for football, and today she proudly tells the episode to her friends. The doctor was right, after all. My feet are the only part of my body that deserve a little more attention:

AFTER A HARD DAY AT PRACTICE, IT FEELS GOOD TO RELAX

just to prevent unnecessary inconvenience and suffering, I have a daily care routine to avoid ingrown toenails. But only that. I also enjoy having a foot massage which, incidentally, is not too unpleasant. After the games, my feet ache, for I am frequently stepped on, but nothing a good massage cannot solve. In fact, my ankles are the only thing that do not fool anyone about the true nature of my profession.

So, I do not take excessive care over my body. I go to bed early, I try to eat healthily and in moderation. If I swim, and play tennis and ping-pong, I do it for pure pleasure, and also because it helps me to fill my time in Manchester, between training.

I like to feel
good with
my body

RESTING IS A
KEY WORD
FOR MY DAYS,
SINCE IT IS
ESSENTIAL
FOR THIS
PROFESSION

LEARNING IS ITS OWN REWARD

NIGHT HAS ALREADY FALLEN, AND WE ARE STILL LIT ONLY BY CANDLELIGHT. THE MOVIE WE PLANNED TO WATCH IN OUR HOME CINEMA WILL HAVE TO BE SEEN TOMORROW. I OWN A REASONABLE AND VARIED COLLECTION OF MOVIES, SO I RARELY GO TO THE CINEMA. AT HOME I CAN WATCH WHATEVER MOVIE I WANT, WHEN I WANT, WITHOUT HAVING TO COPE WITH SCHEDULES AND ALSO WITHOUT BEING SEEN IN PUBLIC.

It truly fits in with the tranquillity I cherish so much. Precisely because I have this option, I watch many movies. I enjoy horror movies because I like the surprise-factor, feeling those shivers down my spine, I like the unpredictable, and the constant uneasiness that is always present in such movies. But I also value a good laugh. Laughing is one of my favourite pastimes, and I do appreciate good comedies, but not just that. As with my music, I have broadened my tastes to include most film genres, such as action and romance movies. In fact, I am only picky when it comes to the quality of the film, not to its genre. I am a cinema lover, but even after thinking about it for a long time, I still cannot choose one single movie that impressed me more deeply than the rest.

Exceptionally, today we have no films, or television. I cannot say I am a dedicated spectator, or a TV show fan, but I like to watch a few shows. I used to watch "Who Wants To Be A Millionaire" and these days I see the contest "One Versus 100" that is on every day on the public Portuguese TV channel, RTP1. The questions presented to the contestants were from a wide range of subjects, testing their general knowledge. I also like to be tested. By nature I am a curious person, who enjoys knowledge and learning. I am fascinated by learning new things, not only related to my professional activity, but also culture. I get carried away by educational shows, which work simultaneously as entertainment, for I always end up learning something new.

At home, all of us play the part of contestants. I think that happens with many families all around the world, wherever there are contests of this kind. It is nothing extraordinary. When the family is together we have a good time, and even make bets on the questions that are asked. As soon as the question is asked we hurry to answer it, and until the correct answer is revealed we argue, each one defending their point of view. I do not like to lose. Therefore, when I think that I am right and someone questions my answer, I run to the computer to search the Internet to end the argument once and for all. "I was right, I was right!" I yell, rejoicing. That is what happened the last time that Zé, Nuno and I watched one of these shows.

The subject was geography. The question was, where is the Laurissilva Forest located, which is considered to be a UNESCO World Heritage site, "I think it is in Madeira," I immediately said. "No it is not" Nuno replied. "Honestly, I don't know," Zé remarked. "Do you want to see if I'm right?" I asked and ran to the computer. "It's in Madeira, it is," I exclaimed. "It's in the

I DO NOT KNOW THE ENTIRE TRUTH, NEITHER DOES MY KNOWLEDGE COVER ALL SUBJECTS

Madeira National Park and it occupies 20 per cent of the island," I explained, while I absorbed all the information I had in front of me on my computer's monitor. I do not know the entire truth, neither does my knowledge cover all subjects, but in this case I felt I was right. Internet search engines give me important additional information, which I try hard to memorise, for I am aware that it enriches my general knowledge and contributes towards my education and intellectual development. I act precisely in the same manner when a word is being discussed, and what its meaning might be, especially when I hear a word that is new to me. So, as I am very curious to know its meaning, I search for all the information I can, then the strange word becomes part of my vocabulary.

THIS IS AN OLD HABIT, VIEWING THE MOST
RECENT GAME MANCHESTER UNITED PLAYED

ANTI-SMOKING

SINCE THE POWER IS STILL NOT ON, AND NIGHT HAS FALLEN, WE TALK FOR A WHILE BEFORE I CLIMB THE STAIRS TO MY ROOM.

EVERYTHING IS ALREADY TIDED UP, FOR IF THERE IS SOMETHING I LOATHE IT IS AN UNTIDY HOUSE. NUNO IS SMOKING AT THE KITCHEN'S WINDOW, FOR THAT IS THE ONLY PLACE IN MY HOUSE WHERE ANYONE IS ALLOWED TO INDULGE IN THAT TERRIBLE HABIT, EVEN THEN WITH A LOT OF GOODWILL FROM ME.

I admit I am anti-tobacco. The sight of a smoker is almost as despicable as the sensation of having to put up with other people's smoke. When I am in a public place, I have no choice but to bear the smoke of those around me – even though, fortunately, recent measures being taken in order to introduce smoking restrictions in all public places are already in force in England. But there is no smoking in my house. I do not deserve to be contaminated inside my own house, and I do not allow it. Either I complain at those who have forgotten this, or else I go to another room. I do not like it, I never did, and it bothers me a lot. Even allowing a small restricted smoking area, by the kitchen window, is benevolent on my part. But, with the rain and cold that are usual outside the house, I do not want to be that cruel. So, there is Nuno beside the window, which must be open, blowing smoke out into the garden.

My bed awaits me, for I do not like to sleep less than eight hours a night. I usually go to sleep between 11:30 pm to midnight, and get up between 7:30 to 8 am, and I only break this routine occasionally, when the next day is my rest day. On those days, I might go out for dinner, in order to vary the daily routine. I go up to my room, where there are some candles, and I get ready to go to sleep. I realise that tonight I cannot watch MU TV (Manchester United's TV channel, which at midnight always broadcasts the latest club match) to watch the game against Aston Villa. This is an old habit, viewing the most recent game Manchester United played, but I am anxious to analyse both the good and bad of every match. I scrutinise my actions on the field, I look at what I have done, right or wrong. I work out if, in a certain situation, I should have given the ball or risked a dribble, if I should have taken a shot or made a key pass. On that particular game I scored my 13th goal of the season, but I could have scored another. I want to watch, in detail, what happened, to draw my own conclusions and rectify everything I think can be rectified.

I DO NOT DESERVE TO BE CONTAMINATED INSIDE MY OWN HOUSE

DRIBBLES, FREE KICKS AND GOALS

I AM NOT A PERFECTIONIST, BUT I LIKE TO FEEL THAT THINGS ARE DONE WELL.

MORE IMPORTANT THAN THAT, I FEEL AN ENDLESS NEED TO LEARN, TO IMPROVE, TO EVOLVE, NOT ONLY TO PLEASE THE COACH AND THE FANS, BUT ALSO TO FEEL SATISFIED WITH MYSELF. IT IS MY CONVICTION THAT THERE ARE NO LIMITS TO LEARNING, AND THAT IT CAN NEVER STOP, NO MATTER WHAT OUR AGE.

Evolution occurs at a daily pace, and covers all aspects of a human being's life. As far as I am concerned, I wish to mature even more, as a player. I want to gain experience and to acquire more knowledge. Every person can be better than they are at the present moment. I know that I can be better. Therefore I try to learn more and more and put what I learn to use year upon year.

I can, for instance, learn how to express myself correctly in English, and I may still learn French. In my professional capacity, I can score more goals and make more key passes. The goals I have scored are a consequence of the confidence I try to improve every

THE GOALS I HAVE SCORED ARE A CONSEQUENCE OF THE CONFIDENCE I TRY TO IMPROVE EVERY DAY

day, also the fact that I am able to get into the penalty area more frequently, can be put down as part of my development. The knack of taking free kicks, for instance, grew out of my own persistence, when I was still a boy starting to play football: I began trying on my own initiative, again and again, and I realised I might even be good at it, so the coaches started to encourage me even more to practise those moves.

Usually at the end of training, I would stay and shoot at goal, persistent and always preoccupied about improving my technique with every move I made. I continued to work on that aspect of my game with both Sporting and Manchester United.

Each football player has an individual style, and I have mine. Thanks to a lot of work and my desire for perfection, I have a technique of my own for taking direct free kicks. The secret? I will not reveal it, for I would be giving a trump card to my opponents . . . I can state only that the success or failure at the moment of taking the free kick is directly related to the position of the body, the way one runs towards

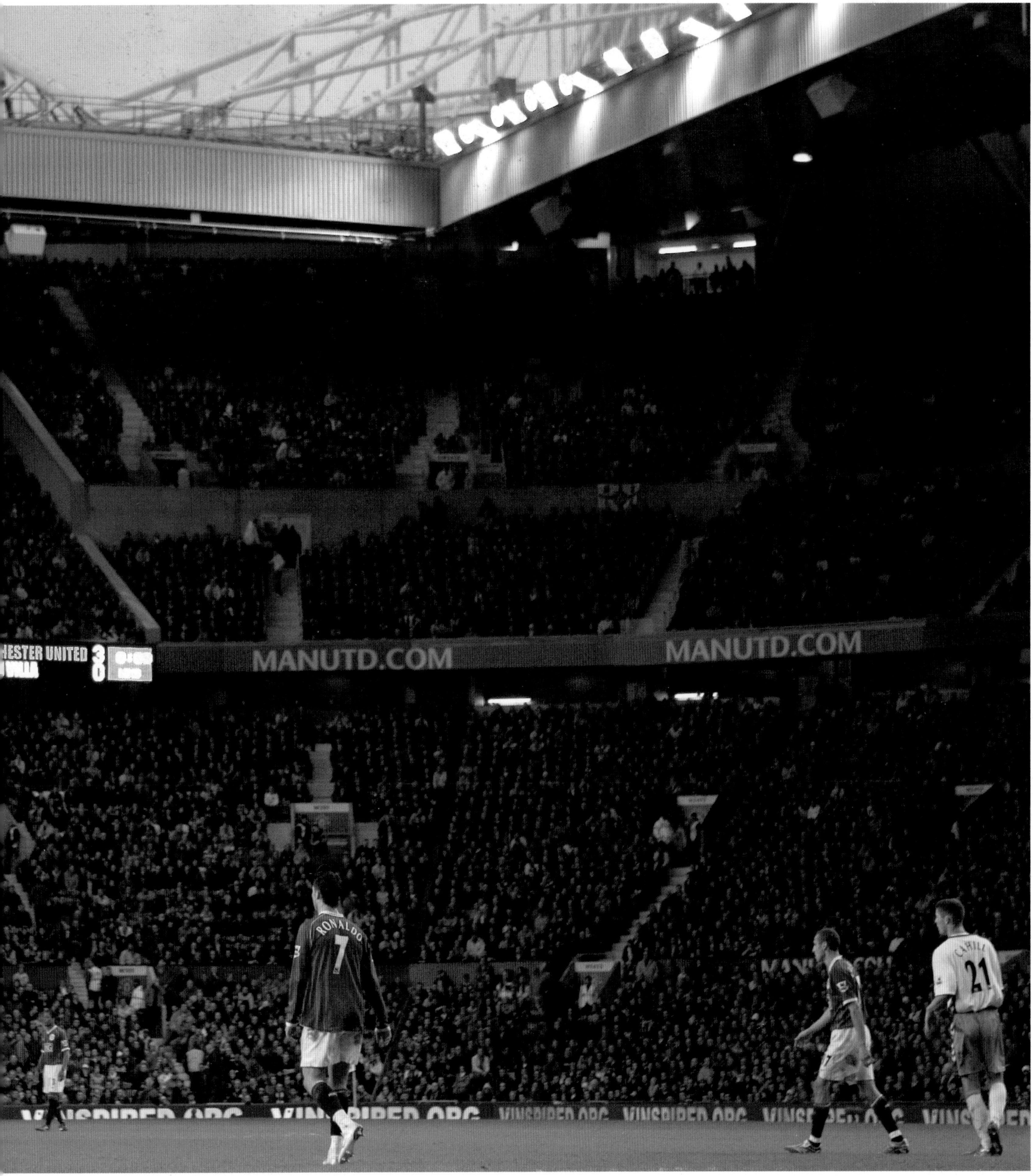
MANUTD.COM
MANUTD.COM
RONALDO
7
CAHILL
21

Absolute
concentration,
even when
circumstances
are adverse . . .

. . . translates
into . . .
goals!!

I WANT TO DEVELOP IN EVERY WAY, NOT JUST IN A SPECIFIC ASPECT

the ball and the way one positions one's feet. At that moment, I think only about which side of the net I am going to aim for. I look at the ball, I look at the net and I say to myself: "take the kick, Ronaldo," then I shoot. Some times it ends well, other times not so well. At Manchester United we have Giggs – who is very good at taking the free kicks – Rooney, and me. In the Portuguese national team, besides myself, there is Simão, Deco and Petit. It all depends on where the foul was committed and the area of the field where that particular player excels in their own speciality of direct free kicks.

A similar thing occurs with my dribbling, which happen by pure instinct. The technique I have today I was born with – giving me the nickname "Abelhinha" (Little Bee) when I was in Andorinha – but obviously it has been perfected over the years. I practise dribbles non-stop during training, and later I try to apply them to the game, but I do not do it at home. Do not think that I spend my days with a ball, inventing this or that dribble. What comes from my feet comes out naturally. Obviously, if I am somewhere and there is a ball, I immediately start kicking it and playing with it, because I have the "itch". But dribbles happen by instinct.

I want to develop in every way, not just in a specific aspect. When a person is ambitious, they will never feel satisfied with what they have, with what they do, or even worse, with what they have done. The past is past. What matters is the present, as it is also important to acquire more grounding for the future. The important thing is aiming to do even better, and becoming even better. Learning and evolving are my mottos for life. That is why I deeply value mixing with people who are more experienced. For it is by this method that I learn something new. Even as little as that might be, I am sure that it is worth it, for I become a little richer. The awareness that I am a public figure leads me to feed this desire for constant improvement because I know that many people look up to me, they point at my success and wish to follow in my footsteps. And I want to be a good example.

THANKS TO A LOT OF WORK AND MY DESIRE FOR PERFECTION, I HAVE A TECHNIQUE OF MY OWN FOR TAKING DIRECT FREE KICKS. THE SECRET?

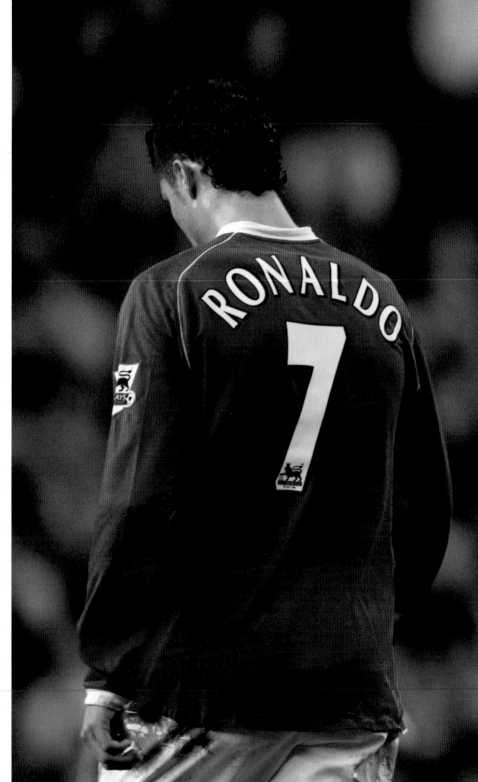

GOING DOWN IN HISTORY AS BOTH A PROFESSIONAL AND A HUMAN BEING

FROM OCTOBER 2006 TO MARCH 2007 A VOTING PROCESS TOOK PLACE IN PORTUGAL, ON A NATIONAL LEVEL, FOR THE ELECTION OF THE GREATEST PERSONALITY IN THE HISTORY OF PORTUGAL, WHETHER ALIVE OR DEAD. THE INITIATIVE CAME FROM RTP1, SIMULTANEOUSLY PROMOTING AN ENTERTAINMENT SHOW, NAMED "THE GREAT PORTUGUESE", WHICH ALSO HAD A CULTURAL, DOCUMENTARY AND INFORMATIVE COMPONENT. I CANNOT FIND THE WORDS TO EXPRESS WHAT I FELT AT THE MOMENT I KNEW THAT MY NAME WAS PART OF A LIST OF 100 PUBLIC FIGURES CONSIDERED AS "THE GREATEST PORTUGUESE OF ALL TIME".

Standing side by side with historical personalities such as D. Afonso Henriques, the first king of Portugal, Fernando Pessoa, Luís de Camões or Bocage, who were poets, Miguel Torga or Almeida Garrett, writers, Gil Vicente, playwright, Gago Coutinho, explorer, Alberto João Jardim, Jorge Sampaio or Cavaco Silva, politicians, among many other individuals who helped to forge Portugal into what it is today, left me truly stunned. To be so young – I had not yet turned 22 when the list was subject to a vote – and to be included already amongst the historical figures of my country, was a great, great honour. I was more than surprised, but I also realised the extent of my responsibilities, and how much people expected of me. That automatically worked as another strong motivation for continuing to work hard, with the same dedication and passion I still feel today.

I believe I ended in 69th place. But that is absolutely irrelevant. It does not matter in what position I was on that list of the 100 Great Portuguese. What was truly important was being surrounded by the most outstanding figures in the history of Portugal and to be considered one of them.

I feel I still have a long journey ahead, if I want to be part of another history: the history of world football. I know it is very difficult, even daring, but I am a persistent, optimistic person, and a fighter, I therefore live in hope of achieving that goal one day. Just as happened to Bobby Charlton, George Best, Maradona or Pelé, amongst many others. They were the best, and they are still remembered for it. I do not compare myself to them, but I would like to leave an impression on my profession. I would like people to remember Cristiano Ronaldo. I want to be remembered as a great football player, but also as a great human being, someone who is respected by everyone. Even today, I feel that people are very fond of me, but I also feel that I still have a long way to go. With a lot of hard work, dedication, and a lot of humility as well, who knows whether that may be possible? I like to think it will and I will try to strive for that.

I have already had some remarkable moments in my career: for instance the day I started in the first team at Sporting, the day I signed for Manchester United, the first goal I scored for them, the day I was first selected for the Portuguese national team, the first European Championship I participated in, my first World Cup . . . Fortunately, I have had more joy than sadness. And I hope for more.

MEDIA EXPOSURE

"WHEN WILL THE DAY COME, THAT I WILL WALK THE STREETS AND BE RECOGNISED BY PEOPLE?"

This was a question I frequently asked my friends, when no one knew who Cristiano Ronaldo yet was. Anonymity, I now find, can be very sweet. I do not refer to the fans' interest, which is a perfectly natural phenomenon, and I never deny them an autograph or a pose for a photograph. I am referring to the many stories that are made up involving my name. However, I recognise that I have previously been more concerned about media exposure than I am today. I reached a certain moment in my life (I believe about two years ago) when I thought: "If I believe everything they say about me, I will live my life gagged and depressed. No, life does not have to be like that."

I stopped evaluating certain situations, for I know people will always either criticise or applaud, that is to say,

opinions will always be different, and never convergent. I respect opinions about my performance on the field, whether I played well or not, whether I scored a good or bad goal, if I involved myself enough or not. I will even listen to the opinions of strangers about these subjects, for I am also curious to know what they think about me as a football professional. But if the subject is my friend A or B, the girlfriend who, after all, is not a girlfriend, the car I bought, or did not buy, then I am not the slightest bit interested, because I have simply given up paying attention to these kinds of stories. I reached this state after concluding that these digressions about my personal life are not going anywhere. This is the price of media interest. But this is the profession I chose, and I do not regret it for a second.

A KID LIKE ANY OTHER

WHEN I LOOK IN THE MIRROR, I SEE A PERSON JUST LIKE SO MANY OTHERS. I SEE SOMEONE WHO REALLY APPRECIATES FUN AND A GOOD LAUGH. I SEE A PERSON WHO LOATHES LIES, WHO DOES NOT LIKE TO BE LATE FOR AN APPOINTMENT, AND WHO, NATURALLY, ALSO DOES NOT LIKE TO HAVE TO WAIT FOR LONG. I ALSO SEE SOMEONE WHO FEELS DISGUSTED BY DISLOYALTY — AND THIS DOES NOT APPLY EXCLUSIVELY TO A RELATIONSHIP BETWEEN A MAN AND A WOMAN — AND WHO CANNOT BEAR TO LOSE ANYTHING. I SEE A PERSON WHO VALUES THE COMPANY OF FRIENDS, WHO ENJOYS BEAUTY AND INTELLIGENCE, WHO FEELS COMFORTABLE AROUND LIVELY AND FUNNY PEOPLE, WHO ENJOYS SHARING AND WHO LIKES TO DREAM.

I ALSO SEE A FUNNY BOY, WHO DOES PRACTICALLY EVERYTHING THAT PEOPLE HIS AGE DO, ALTHOUGH HE MUST BE A BIT MORE CAREFUL, AND THE INEVITABLE SENSE OF RESPONSIBILITY THAT COMES WITH THE FACT OF BEING CONSIDERED A PUBLIC FIGURE. MANY ARE THOSE WHO, ALL THROUGH MY CAREER, HAVE ASKED ME THIS QUESTION. IT IS NOT AT ALL TRUE. I MIGHT NOT DO EXACTLY THE SAME, BUT I ALLOW MYSELF DIFFERENT TYPES OF PLEASURES THAT MAY NOT BE WITHIN THE REACH OF THE MAJORITY. IT IS TRUE I DO NOT OFTEN GO TO DISCOS, BECAUSE I KNOW THAT RESTING IS ESSENTIAL TO MY JOB, BUT AS FOR THE REST I AM NOT TOO DIFFERENT FROM THE BOYS OF MY GENERATION. THE TRUTH IS, I TRY TO BE A PERFECTLY NORMAL YOUNG MAN.

THE MIRROR ALSO REVEALS A CHILD. I AM A CHILD, WITH PRIDE, AND I WILL DO ANYTHING TO REMAIN AS SUCH. AGE, IN MY OPINION, IS JUST A DETAIL, AND AN IRRELEVANT ONE. THE CHARM OF LIFE IS IN FULLY PRESERVING THAT CHILDISH ASPECT, FOR ONLY IN THAT WAY WILL WE FACE SETBACKS MORE EASILY, AND MORE OPTIMISTICALLY. IN TRUTH, THAT IS THE ONLY WAY TO BE HAPPY. BUT I WANT TO BE A CHILD WHO LISTENS TO THE ADVICE GIVEN BY THOSE WHO ARE OLDER ACCORDING TO THEIR YEARS. I RECENTLY READ A BOOK ABOUT TWO MEN MEETING. ONE OF THEM WAS 110 YEARS OLD, AND HAD AN IMMENSE LIFE STORY TO TELL, BUT HIS EYES REVEALED A BRIGHT GLOW AND GREAT PURENESS, NOT THE TRACES OF AGE. FOR HE SIMPLY DID NOT ALLOW THE SUM OF HIS YEARS TO BE REFLECTED IN HIS GESTURES, IN HIS DEMEANOUR, IN HIS WAY OF LIFE. I IDENTIFIED MYSELF WITH THIS EXAMPLE OF JOVIALITY. FOR THIS REASON I STATE THAT AGE IS BUT A DETAIL. THE CHILD WITHIN ALL OF US MUST NEVER DIE. I WILL NOT ALLOW THAT TO HAPPEN TO ME, NOT EVEN WHEN I AM 60, 70, 80 OR 90 YEARS OLD. I WANT TO BE A CHILD FOREVER. I NEVER WANT MY EYES TO STOP SHINING. I ALWAYS WANT TO HAVE A SMILE FOR LIFE.

ENGLAND'S PLAYER OF THE YEAR

ON APRIL 22ND, 2007 I RECEIVED TWO AWARDS THAT FILLED ME WITH PRIDE: ENGLAND'S BEST PLAYER OF THE YEAR AND BEST YOUNG PLAYER OF THE YEAR. I FELT EVEN MORE HONOURED BECAUSE BOTH DISTINCTIONS WERE THE RESULT OF A VOTE BY THE PROFESSIONAL FOOTBALLERS ASSOCIATION, WHICH ONLY ONCE IN THE HISTORY OF THE PREMIER LEAGUE HAD AWARDED BOTH TROPHIES TO THE SAME PLAYER, AND IN THE SAME SEASON: THAT HAPPENED 30 YEARS AGO TO ANDY GRAY, WHO PLAYED FOR ASTON VILLA.

Now it is me who comes after him, and that fact, *per se*, could not leave me unmoved. I make an effort to improve each day that goes by, and this public acknowledgement was a kind of reward, another reward, for all the work I have been doing.

I realise that this season is going well for me: I have scored goals, I have made key passes, Manchester United and I are both doing well. For that reason, I believed in the possibility of winning one of the awards I was nominated for. But the thought of winning both awards, I admit, did not go through my head, for I had worthy competitors. I admit that it surprised me. I only received the good news on the day of the awards, for protocol dictated that before the ceremony I had to pose with the trophies for the cameras and I would also give a few interviews. This was because at the end of the ceremony I needed to leave for the airport immediately, where a plane waited to take me back to Manchester. The game against Milan, for the semi-finals of the Champions' League, would take place two days after that, and I had no time to lose.

It was a lightening trip: I left Manchester around 2:00 pm, and before midnight I was back home again. I was accompanied by some of those who are dear to me, and also by my coach, Alex Ferguson, and that iconic figure that goes by the name of Bobby Charlton. We had already met in Manchester United's dressing room, since he is a constant presence in our club, but the moments we shared on the plane allowed us to talk together in a more deep and intimate manner. We exchanged opinions about the Premier League, about Manchester United's career, about the Champions' League. My admiration for Bobby Charlton was reinforced. If that is still possible.

When I arrived at the hotel where the ceremony took place, I did not waste much time changing clothes. In my daily life I like to wear simple clothing, that is, I prefer sportswear, absolutely casual wear, in which jeans play a prominent role. But occasionally I also like to wear a suit, preferably with no tie. This ceremony required that I took a little more care about my appearance, because I already knew that I was going to receive the awards. I chose a black suit, a white shirt and a bow tie. I went to the ceremony, and at the moment I held both awards for the first time, I offered up a wide smile, full of happiness, while I thought: "Ronaldo, you have to work even harder, to become even better. Nothing ends here. Everything begins here, enough said, this is another step on your path towards maturity."

For most of the time, I kept calm. I only felt somewhat nervous a few moments before my name was announced for the first award of the night, Best Young Player of The Year. But even with the room filled with around a thousand guests, I quickly got past that sensation. It was with a feeling of great joy, honour and pride that I went up to the stage for the first time, and shortly after that for the second time, to receive,

WITH MY FAMILY, MY FRIENDS AND MY COACH AT THE AWARD OF ENGLAND'S ASSOCIATION OF PROFESSIONAL FOOTBALL PLAYERS. I ONLY FELT A LITTLE NERVOUS JUST BEFORE MY NAME WAS ANNOUNCED

from the hands of Alex Ferguson, the trophy for England's Best Player of The Year. I heard him refer to me as "the best football player in the world today", and that statement, coming from him, sent shivers down my spine.

It was undeniably another striking moment in my career. After all the controversy that arose during the Germany World Cup, I managed to show that pressure only makes me stronger. I put myself to the test and I succeeded, and I believe I am proving it. From the beginning of the season I have tried to calm myself down, and wear an icy mask during the games in which whistles abounded. I ignored it, and faced them with an extra motivational factor. I made an effort not to react to provocations, whatever they were. With the help of my family and friends, I try to persist with the process of growing and maturing. The season ended up going very well for me, which leads me to conclude that the attitude I adopted was the right one. The only thing I want is to play football, and play it as well as possible, with a single purpose: the success of Manchester United. Therefore I assure you that the best is yet to come. And the best will be the league titles, which, from my point of view, represent the icing on the cake.

I returned to Manchester with two new awards in my bag, but still humble, and with exactly the same attitude towards life. My thoughts immediately focused on the semi-final of the Champions' League, which was to take place two days later at Old Trafford. On that magnificent stage I scored the first goal of the game, maybe the strangest of my entire career. Milan drew level and then got ahead of us, but we managed to turn the score around and won 3-2. It was another night of glory. And I hope it is repeated many, many times.

BEING THE BEST IN THE WORLD IS NOT AN OBSESSION

IN 2005 I RECEIVED THE AWARD THAT ACCLAIMED ME THE BEST YOUNG FOOTBALL PLAYER IN THE WORLD, BESTOWED ON ME BY VOTES OF FANS THROUGHOUT THE WORLD, AND THIS FILLED ME WITH PLEASURE AND PRIDE.

INDIVIDUAL AWARDS CONSTITUTE AN EXCELLENT INCENTIVE, EVEN FOR THOSE WHO DO NOT NEED IT, ALTHOUGH I BELIEVE TEAM VICTORIES ARE MUCH MORE IMPORTANT. DURING THE LAST FEW MONTHS, I HAVE HEARD MENTIONED, SEVERAL TIMES, THE POSSIBILITY THAT I MIGHT BE CONSIDERED THE BEST FOOTBALL PLAYER IN THE WORLD. THERE ARE THOSE WHO AGREE, AND THOSE WHO DISAGREE.

As for me, that nomination would be a dream come true. However, I do not live with that obsession, I do not think about it when I get up every day for training, nor is it for that award that I perform better (or worse) in each game in which I take part. Whatever has to happen will happen naturally, as a consequence of my evolution process, and also of the success that the club I represent will come to achieve, for this phenomenon can be compared to a snowball that gets larger as it runs its course: if Manchester United is doing well, I will do well; the greater the success of United, the greater the success of each of its players.

I can honestly say that, more important than any individual title, whatever it is, is the feeling that I have achieved the people's acknowledgement: knowing that my work is appreciated, knowing they like my personality and my character, and knowing that they value my professionalism. For this reason, I do not live a life obsessed by the title of Best Player in the World. I want everything to carry on naturally, as it has been until now, for I believe this is the right course. As I have already revealed, I live in hope of always being the best, or one of the best, in whatever I do – and I do not exclusively mean my professional capacity. Anything that I gain beyond that will be extra profit. If, one day, one of those awards is destined for me, it will be welcome and I will be there to receive it. But believe me, it is not that which drives me.

Manchester United was the turning point, not only in my career but also in my life, in view of the media exposure that comes to those who wear this shirt. Being the first Portuguese to play for Manchester United (and I am aware of the club's glorious history) represented, from the first moment, an extra helping of incentive. I did not have to wait long to understand that I was on the right track to

achieve one of my objectives: belonging to the elite of the best players. At the exact moment I put on the "Red Devils" shirt, I felt sure that Manchester United was the ideal club for me, for my development as both a player and as a person. I felt that this was "the" club, that this was "the" country. Almost four years have passed since I first walked onto the iconic Old Trafford pitch. Today I consider it one of my homes. Without a lie I can declare that I feel immense pride and joy at representing this great world club. Hearing praise from presidents, coaches and players from other clubs is always gratifying – who does not enjoy a compliment? – and in some way it is the proof that I am really developing and growing as a football professional. But here at Manchester United is where I feel happy. So much so that I have no problem in saying that I would like to stay for many more years.

I did not forget my country when celebrating my first championship

CHAMPION,
AT LAST

I DO NOT KNOW WHAT IT IS LIKE TO BE A PORTUGUESE CHAMPION, BUT I NOW KNOW WHAT IT IS LIKE TO BE AN ENGLISH CHAMPION. THE LEAST THAT I CAN SAY IS, IT IS SPECTACULAR. MY FRIENDS USED TO SAY, PLAYFULLY – USING A COMMON BRAZILIAN EXPRESSION – "THAT MY FEET HAD NOT YET WARMED UP FOR TITLES".

I SMILED WHEN I LISTENED TO THEM, BECAUSE THERE WAS NO POINT IN OVERRATING SUCH COMMENTS: WINNING IS ONE OF THE GREATEST THINGS, BUT WHEN WE LOSE IT IS NECESSARY TO QUICKLY MOVE ON AND WORK AS HARD AS WE CAN, TO MAKE SUCCESS HAPPEN. IT IS TRUE THAT MY FEET WERE "COLD FOR TITLES". HOWEVER, FROM THIS MOMENT ON, I SUSPECT THAT THEY HAVE WARMED UP. MORE THAN THAT, THEY ARE ON FIRE . . .

On May 6th, 2007, I stayed at home, my eyes glued to the television set. Chelsea were playing against Arsenal, and they could not afford to drop any points. On the day before that, we had beaten Manchester City – I scored the only goal of the game – which meant that, if Chelsea lost or drew, we would automatically be champions. At the start I was calm, and I became even calmer when I watched Boulahrouz being sent off and Arsenal leading, having scored a penalty. "Well, that's it, we're going to be champions," I cried out. But Chelsea drew level, and during the final 15 minutes, Zé and Nuno's stress rubbed off on me. Those were dramatic moments, as my nails, at the time, could confirm. "Isn't this game ever going to end?" I kept repeating, moving restlessly on the couch every time Chelsea launched an attack and created more opportunities on goal. I was worried. Very worried. I had the feeling that time had stopped. The minutes were not going by, the game would not end. "Don't tell me this will only be resolved next week!" I cried out. "No, the game is going to end like this," Zé said, to calm me down. And it certainly did. Chelsea drew, Manchester United were the English champions. I leapt from the sofa, hugged Zé and Nuno, called my mother, we went in the kitchen and opened a bottle of champagne, I called a few friends, received a lot of messages and phone calls, we played music and we celebrated. "It's all over!" I yelled. And I let out an expression we often use at home. "Go and get it!"

A champion! I had just become a champion! The feeling is indescribable, and nothing can compare with it. During my first year at United we won the FA Cup (2003/04), and two years later, the League Cup (2005/06). These two trophies were very important, for winning is an incomparable sensation. But winning the Premier League is different, something unique. Last season, we were close to winning the FA Cup again, but it escaped us at the last moment; in the Portuguese national team I was close, very close to the European title, but it slipped through our fingers in the final against Greece. Luck was not with Manchester United, nor with Portugal. Not winning any titles never really made me feel frustrated. Obviously, I wanted to win championships, but I knew I had a lot of time ahead of me. I was right. That moment finally arrived on a Sunday afternoon.

A CHAMPION! I HAD JUST BECOME A CHAMPION! THE FEELING IS INDESCRIBABLE AND NOTHING CAN COMPARE WITH IT

The progress of Manchester United in the English League has been remarkable. Besides having won extremely important victories, we played a very attractive style of football; we showed strong character, determination and attitude. It is clear that the team has grown in strength; today it is much more mature and experienced. This combination of factors is reflected on the field, and thanks to them we have had a fantastic season. The English title is so incredibly important that only those who have lived the dream of this competition can understand how much the Premier League Title means to the club, to the players, to the fans. Winning it, I can assure you, is more important than winning the Champion's League. For this is truly a championship from another galaxy. And Manchester United, with all its magnificence, could also be considered a club from another universe.

Twenty minutes after Manchester United was officially acclaimed as the new English champions I joined my team-mates in the town centre and together we celebrated in a bar. The party, which featured all the club's chants, was a lot of fun, lasted until dawn and continued the next morning, at the United training centre, in the gym. We were all dead tired, but drunk with happiness.

For the next game, we went to Stamford Bridge with championship status, which, I recognise, had a special feeling. I, and certain other team-mates, did not play, because with the championship decided, it was possible to rest those players. "Have you heard my new chant?" I asked Alex Ferguson on the day of the game with West Ham, the last in the championship, the game after which we were crowned champions, during which I remained on the bench until the second half. "I do," he answered. "He plays on the left, he plays on the right, the boy Ronaldo . . ." and he reproduced the words of the song that fans sing. "No, no", I told him. "The new one is different. Do you want to listen? It goes like this: "he plays on the bench, he plays on the bench . . ." Ferguson could not help himself, and let out a loud laugh. I understood the importance and the need to rotate players, letting those who had played more rest more, towards the end of the season. I understand this, and I always accept his decisions. It is true that I still had a chance of becoming the highest goal scorer in the premiership, but I was never obsessed with that, and so it was not a priority for me. I came in third, after Drogba and McCarthy, but the most important priority had already been achieved.

The atmosphere at Old Trafford is always unique, but on that day it was different. The atmosphere was truly wonderful, and it would be impossible to find any other place where so many were so happy. The fact that we lost the game was irrelevant. The title had returned home. The moment when we lifted the Cup was tremendous. I sprayed champagne over my team-mates, I shouted with joy, I jumped up and down, I felt the weight of that trophy for the first time. I fooled around a lot, and the medal I had received moments before fell onto the pitch, as I hugged Evra.

The sons and nephews of the players had permission to accompany them on the field, during the party. I was next to the Cup, jumping around, when all of a sudden I felt someone jump on my back. I looked and I saw Zé on top of me, and my mother was there, by my side, hugging and kissing me, my brother, Nuno, and Rogério were jumping up and down. It was great. I did not expect them to come down from the stand to join me. That moment of celebration was even more significant. "Listen, Ronny (my nick-name at United), your kids and nephews are a bit big . . ." some of my mates joked.

So it was in the company of my family – my most precious asset – that I went around the stadium, with the Cup in my hands and the Portuguese flag covering my back, because I never forget my country. This was how we were with the supporters, who were singing my chant; this was how we, the Manchester United fans and my family, repeated the dance, our arms raised, to the left ("he plays on the left), and to the right ("he plays on the right"); this was how we jumped around, celebrated, laughed, ran around the field, and rejoiced. We were all dripping wet, from the rain that blessed the ceremony, and with my mother struggling, her high heels digging into the turf. But that did not matter. It was our moment, the fans' moment, the club's staff, the players, the coaches, but also the moment for my family, so I dedicate this title to them. My mother, who was continually by my side until I went into the locker room, received a great compliment from my friend Heinze, who was surprised by her joviality. "Your mother is so young! She's fantastic!" he commented the next day. Obviously I agreed, and was very proud.

This was my best season ever. I was a champion with Manchester United, which was my main objective, I made countless key passes, I scored 23 goals in all competitions in which Manchester United participated, I won all the individual trophies, and there were 16 of them. Among them, I gained an important acknowledgement from the United supporters and from my team-mates, who elected me player of the year. However, nothing can be compared to the unforgettable sensation of being a champion, in what I consider to have been the highest point in my career. The boy who one day left his island and his family, in search of a dream, had finally achieved his moment of glory. At the instant I raised the Cup the boy was there, on the field, and he was the happiest boy on Earth.

I RAISED THE CUP TO MY FAMILY. I WAS THE HAPPIEST BOY ON EARTH

WHO KNOWS
WHAT THE FUTURE
MAY BRING . . .

First published in Great Britain 2007 by Macmillan
an imprint of Pan Macmillan Ltd
in association with Ideias & Rumos – Edições Limitada

Pan Macmillan, 20 New Wharf Road, London N1 9RR
Basingstoke and Oxford
Associated companies throughout the world
www.panmacmillan.com

ISBN 978-0-230-70669-9

Originally published 2007 as *Momentos* by Ideias & Rumos – Edições Limitada, Portugal

Picture Acknowledgements
Jorge Monteiro, exceptions: pages 48, 56, 66, 98, 114 Cristiano Ronaldo; pages 103, 105 Gestifute Media;
pages 52, 53, 56, 57, 58, 59, 60, 61 Jornal "O Jogo"; page 26
Banco Espírito Santo; page 27 Coca-Cola; pages 30, 31 Pepe Jeans; pages 38, 39
Nike; pages 68, 71 Manchester United; page 6 Getty Images.

9 8 7 6 5 5 4 3 2 1

A CIP catalogue record for this book is available from
the British Library.

Coordinator: Luís Correia
Author: Cristiano Ronaldo, with Manuela Brandão
Photographer: Jorge Monteiro
Design: Rui Guimarães
Translation: Lígia Santos Rodrigues and Paula Pereira
English Editor: Derek Reece
Printing: Butler and Tanner

Visit **www.panmacmillan.com** to read more about all our books
and to buy them. You will also find features, author interviews and
news of any author events, and you can sign up for e-newsletters
so that you're always first to hear about our new releases.